Prime Mincer

1.3

Winter 2011

Subscriptions: $27 for 1 year (3 issues). Inquire for international and institutional rates.

Submissions are accepted year round.

For more info regarding subscriptions, submissions, general rants, raves or anything else, please visit the website.

www.primemincer.com

ISBN-13: 978-0615589978
ISSN-10: 0615589979

"Damselfly" by Pinckney Benedict originally appeared in *Surreal South '11* published by Press 53.

Cover Design by Bryan Estes

Peter Lucas—Managing Editor
Abby Wheetley—Fiction Editor
Amy Graziano—Poetry Editor
Sequoia Nagamatsu—Interviews Editor
Jessica Easto—Proofreader, Master of Chicago Style, Hater of Double Spaces After Periods.

The editors would like to give special thanks to Rodney Jones for judging the first annual poetry contest and also for always being amazingly available to his students. He's a good egg...

Also, as always, we would like to thank Dexter Wheetley, Emily Wheetley, and Jacob Lucas. You kids rock.

Contents

A Shrine To His Ancestors

Zhang Fengqi kneels before the low table in the corner. Left of center, he assembles a pyramid of oranges: a triangle of three and one nesting on top. He lifts and dusts with his sleeve a photograph of Maddie, his late wife and the mother of his two sons. In the picture, one he'd taken on their honeymoon trip to Chicago, her blond hair swirls around her face, and she is hugging her jacket to keep it tight against the wind. Her smile is wide. He remembers the moment. They were happy, he deliriously so. Before the wedding, her mother had been angry that she was marrying Fengqi (not, he later realized, because he was Chinese, but because he was other—any other). And his parents were thousands of miles away in Shanghai, equally disappointed in his choice. But at that moment, clowning in front of the larger-than-life lions of the Art Institute, they didn't care what anyone else thought.

He replaces that picture on the table and picks up another. This one is of his mother, who died years ago. He believes the photograph was taken by his father on the Bund in Shanghai, but the blurry crowd in the background could have arisen anywhere in that dense city. She is stiffly posed, aware of the camera and forcing a smile; her gray-streaked hair is pulled back. A dull blue jacket in the old Party style makes her shoulders look wide and strong, which Fengqi knows they were not. There's also an older sepia print of his father and mother together in what might be their wedding finery. The last photograph, of his father, is more recent, taken after he'd moved here to D.C. from China just last year. Fengqi wishes he had chosen a different picture, because here his father looks nervous and uncomfortable, as if thinking he should have remained in Shanghai to finish his days among the bones of his forebears, but in all the other snapshots he appears drawn and sick, with the inevitable too clearly published on his tired face.

Fengqi lights the stick of incense, watches the drifting string of smoke rise, and inhales the scent of sandalwood that he will forever associate with his father. The shrine had been the old man's creation, his link to the ancient ways. Fengqi doesn't believe in such things. And yet, the memories abide here and they comfort him. He bows to the pictures, and rises.

From next door comes a steady hammering noise: the long-delayed renovation project in his neighbor's apartment. A gaping hole in the brick wall facing the alley, the origin of which Fengqi no longer remembers, is to be repaired and a balcony installed. The balcony seems unsafe for Susanna's baby, who will soon begin to crawl, but Fengqi understands (because six-year-old Simon has told him this) that Aloysius plans to sell the apartment and move, with Susanna and little Loyal, to a quieter, safer community. Which, Fengqi supposes, would be anywhere that Thomas—the father of the baby and the man with whom Susanna used to live, and who even now often sits in his parked car on M Street watching the building—is less likely to follow. And if he does follow, like the hungry ghost of Chinese legends, what then?

Claudia, their neighbor and, lately, the boys' sitter, enters with Simon and Wesley, who both run to Fengqi to show him what they have found on their walk. Simon presents him with a handful of leaves, ordinary maple and oak leaves that show signs of the changing season, still green but gold and red at the edges. Wesley clutches a dandelion that he holds under his chin, as Claudia has apparently instructed him.

"Yellow," says Wesley.

"It certainly is," says Fengqi.

"They both wanted to bring you presents," Claudia says.

Fengqi would be lost without Claudia, a former marketing consultant who has taken readily to childcare and now seems content only when she's around the boys. These past months, as his father sank out of reach, Fengqi had struggled to care for Simon and Wesley, just as he had after Maddie's car accident. When he'd married Jessica, a second-generation Chinese-American with her own family ties to the old country, he thought she'd be able to help more, that they would face his father's death together and carry the boys through yet another loss. That wasn't why he married her; he just thought it would be so. But she's been distracted, busy with her work, and more uncomfortable with the boys, and they with her, than he'd hoped. He believes harmony will come in time, because that's what his father had taught him. He just doesn't know when.

Now there is high-pitched barking in the hallway and they all—Fengqi, Claudia, and the boys—go to investigate the commotion. Charles and Craig, from Number 1, reunited after a brief separation, are assembled there with their pug Sascha and a new dog they have named Mole, pronounced, Claudia has explained because it is a Spanish word Fengqi doesn't understand, "molay." The new dog is meant to keep Sascha company and to replace—if replacement is the right notion, which Fengqi knows it is not—their first pug who, Charles and Craig maintain, was dog-napped.

Shelley, Mr. Artoyen's buxom new wife, comes out of their apartment, shushing as she eases the door shut, because Sam, as he insists everyone call him now that he is just one of the residents instead of being the building's developer, is recovering from the heart attack he suffered while they were moving in. The painter, the wiry little man with the grey eyes, peeks out of his unit, releasing a wave of paint fumes that bites at Fengqi's nose. The man emerges, carrying a painting—awkwardly balanced on his hip, arms stretched to their limits because it is a long, wide canvas—that he lifts onto oversized hooks that have been empty for months. Aiding in this effort—mostly by judging from afar whether the canvas hangs level—is the tall sculptor from Number 3 whose ubiquitous cigarette dangles, unlit, from his mouth. The work looks familiar to Fengqi, as if the painter has recreated the piece that once hung in that spot, an indecipherable abstract roofline under an impossibly blue sky.

The chaos in the hallway gallery reminds Fengqi of the day his mother-in-law—Maddie's mother—had arrived unannounced, the day of his first date with Jessica, the day his father remembered

10

was the anniversary of the Nanjing Massacre. The day Fengqi realized that, no matter how much he planned, no matter how settled he thought he was, his life was an ocean of change over which he had no control.

And just as this thought occurs to him, he sees through the gallery's glass doors a yellow cab pull up and Mrs. Martin emerge, as if his memory has conjured her appearance. He has forgotten that she was due, but regular visits are now her custom. Despite his marriage to Jessica, she has been coming each month since his father's funeral, whether because his death foretells her own and she wishes to make the most of the time remaining to her, or because she genuinely wants to help, he can't be sure. It hardly matters. The boys see her now, pull the door open and welcome her with noisy hugs and kisses, which she tolerates with grace that a year ago was unthinkable. She greets Fengqi by patting his forearm with a gloved hand.

The door to the building's front apartment opens and now, he thinks, the tableau will be complete, exactly as it was that day. But of course the young couple who once lived there is a couple no more and have left that apartment. It is the famous novelist who lives there now, the writer who, Jessica has told him, has a great book that is about to be published. At this time last year the man was in Paris, but his return to Nanking Mansion has sown more change, more chaos. Instead of the novelist emerging from the apartment, as Fengqi expects, however, it is Jessica who closes the door behind her.

Jessica and Mrs. Martin stand face to face. The two women are roughly the same height, but the similarity ends there. Jessica's black hair hangs straight to her shoulders, and her dark complexion is, or to Fengqi's eye appears to be, without makeup. Mrs. Martin's hair is gray, rigidly swirled above her head like a crown, and her powdered face is pale. Jessica wears jeans and a T-shirt. Mrs. Martin is in a black suit. If there is resentment between them, neither has said so to Fengqi. And yet they do not speak. They simply nod.

And then the commotion in the gallery dissipates. Charles and Craig and the dogs depart for their afternoon walk; the painter, his new work now hanging, returns to his studio, as does the sculptor. The hammering from the back of the building has ceased, along with the crying. And Claudia and Mrs. Martin herd Simon and Wesley into the Zhangs' apartment for a promised snack and a glimpse at the presents their grandmother has brought. Only Fengqi and Jessica remain.

"You were in the writer's apartment," Fengqi says. He has learned in his few months of marriage to Jessica that questions are often misinterpreted, and so he usually speaks to her in statements. He doesn't mean to accuse her. He only seeks confirmation of a fact.

"You saw me come out," Jessica says.

"He was there." Although in intonation this is also a statement, in his mind he is asking a question. He didn't see the writer. He doesn't know whether it is true.

"We were going over his manuscript one last time."

Jessica has told him that the book is done. When she quit her job at the bookstore—she said after her hysterectomy that she couldn't stand the way people looked at her there, a young woman who was no longer a woman—she began working with the writer to help him finish his book about atrocities. She has told Fengqi that part of the book involves China, especially the Japanese massacre of Chinese civilians at Nanjing in 1937. Fengqi knows about this incident, of course. His father survived it although he never talked about it. The massacre is part of his own family history and he doesn't understand why it should be put in a book of fiction.

"The book is finished." A question and a statement.

"Some last minute things," she says.

"He depends on you."

"He says he does, yes."

"Then it's good you are there to help him."

Fengqi has arranged for Claudia to watch the boys after school, because he had anticipated that Jessica would be back at work. And because Claudia needed the money—having lost her husband and her job at the same time, and very nearly losing her condo as a result. And because she got along well with the boys. It had seemed like an ideal situation, despite the expense. He's been thinking, though, that Jessica's recent moroseness might be due in part to her own unemployment and having few responsibilities around the house. He has been doing most of the cooking, he was caring for his father, he even cleaned. He doesn't blame her for not wanting to continue at the bookstore, although she had in the past claimed to enjoy it there. He has assured her that he fully understands, but the truth is that he does not. He has even tried to talk to her about this, but she deflects him. Now, though Claudia will be unhappy, he is thinking that Jessica should at least watch the children after school. Her work with the novelist is flexible. She has the time.

Jessica phones him at work. Simon's teacher has called the apartment and wants to meet with them as soon as possible. The next afternoon they go together to pick Simon up from school and they sit in his classroom, in the tiny schoolhouse chairs, with Mrs. Praisner standing above them like a looming, tweedy giant. Simon waits with a teacher's aide on the playground.

"I'm afraid he's been fighting," says Mrs. Praisner.

"That's not like Simon," Fengqi says.

"Lately, I'm afraid it is. He hit another boy because of something he said."

"Said what?"

"That Simon's mother is dead."

"As you know, she died in an accident, a little over a year ago."

"What he said exactly was, 'Your mother's dead and she's not coming back.' And that's when Simon punched him."

The incident at the school gives Fengqi the idea that the

time has come to move. Originally, Maddie had chosen this building in this neighborhood because she wanted to expose the boys to diversity and to the arts, and Fengqi had agreed, with some reluctance, that they would benefit. But he's no longer certain they were right. Although the neighborhood has seen improvement, it still seems dangerous, and, after Simon had admitted to Fengqi that a teenager had stolen his watch in the alley, the boys were no longer allowed to wander outside by themselves. It's no place for children, or at least not his children, and he worries about Jessica's safety, too. Isn't an attractive young woman vulnerable?

Without telling Jessica—he understands that this is a risk, that she would prefer to be consulted on a matter this important, but he believes she will enjoy the surprise—Fengqi begins looking at houses in the far suburb of Annandale with the help of a local Chinese-American realtor, second generation, like Jessica. There is a large population of Asians in the area, an abundance of Asian groceries and restaurants, plus public schools where Simon and Wesley won't feel out of place and Jessica can make friends. She'll come to love the area, and so will they.

He sees three that he thinks will work. Before he can discuss the move with Jessica, however, one of the houses is taken off the market and the second is sold. The realtor is blunt: he must act fast.

Fengqi is in Philadelphia for a conference at which he is presenting the data from a new report to be issued by his bureau in the Labor Department. It is the first time he has left the boys with Jessica overnight, and he didn't want to do it, but the conference is important. And she's their mother now; they must all grow to love each other, sooner rather than later. He tries not to worry.

He is waiting his turn to deliver his presentation when his cell phone rings. He's aware of the stares he draws as he tries to silence the phone and escape the auditorium. In the anteroom, he answers the call from Claudia. He listens, hears static on the line and something in Claudia's voice—it's pitched high, and, while she's normally calm and methodical, now she's speaking so fast it's hard for him to understand—alarms him. She's in the emergency room at G.W. Hospital with Wesley who's running a high fever. She doesn't know where Jessica is. She had knocked on the novelist's door, because she often goes there to work on the man's book, but there was no answer. Claudia hadn't known what else to do.

Fengqi leaves the conference. There isn't time to tell anyone; he just gathers his belongings, checks out of the hotel, and goes.

While he's en route, Claudia calls with updates. Doctors suspect a virus. Still no word from Jessica. They're giving him antibiotics. Susanna from next door has agreed to watch Simon when he gets home from school. Wesley is resting, and they're going home. Fengqi changes course and heads for Nanking Mansion.

The apartment is quiet when Fengqi enters. His arms ache from his tight grip on the steering wheel, and his leg is stiff from the steady pressure on the gas pedal as he sped down I-95. Jessica is sitting in the kitchen, sipping tea, lit only by the lamp over the stove.

"Wesley's okay," he says. He doesn't go to her. The overnight bag still in his hand anchors him.

"Yes. He's fine. Sleeping"

"I was worried."

"He's fine now."

"Claudia couldn't find you."

"I was working."

"I was worried."

"I'm sorry," Jessica says. "But everything's fine."

"No," Fengqi says. "I don't think it is." He hears that his voice is too loud, that anger, an emotion he seldom expresses, is burning in him, like Wesley's fever. He turns away.

They go out to eat at their favorite restaurant, Mario's, leaving the boys with Claudia. Since the scare of Wesley's fever, which passed as quickly as it arose, they've spoken little, and Fengqi thinks they need to take this break. He wishes they could go away

15

somewhere, just the two of them, on a kind of honeymoon, like the trip he and Maddie took to Chicago, but that's out of the question because of work and the boys. So a night out will have to do, for now. Jessica is staring at the menu and doesn't answer when the waiter asks for their orders, but when Fengqi chooses the shrimp scampi, she tells the waiter she'll have the same. Fengqi looks at her. She never eats shrimp. She never orders the same thing he does.

He says, "There's something I wanted to talk about," at the same time that she says, "We need to talk." He smiles at the coincidence, but she doesn't.

"You first," she says. She sips her water.

"All right. I thought we could save a little money if you watched the boys after school, instead of paying Claudia to do it." He feels badly for Claudia, who needs the money they pay her, but he'll help her find something else that will make better use of her experience in advertising.

Jessica nods, still holding the water glass to her lips, but Fengqi has the impression that she isn't listening.

"There's something else," he says.

And then he tells her he's made an offer on a house.

"*Hao ma?*" Is that okay? Since his father's death, Jessica has stopped studying Chinese. He wants her to keep using it, for the boys' sakes, and so for simple expressions he sometimes slips into Mandarin. "*Hao bu hao?*" Okay or not?

She nods again. They sit silently while the food is set in front of them. Jessica stares at her shrimp.

"The thing is, now that the book is done," she says, "Nathan is moving back to Paris."

For a moment, Fengqi is pleased with the implication of Nathan's impending move and he smiles—one less thing to worry about, nothing to interfere with their move to the suburbs, and with that distraction out of the way Jessica will have plenty of time for the boys—until he realizes, as if he is hearing the delayed report of a distant gun, what is coming next.

16

"He's asked me to go with him."

Has he heard right? The restaurant is loud. Did he misunderstand?

"Why would he ask this of you? The work is done, you said. For the next book he can find another...helper."

"It's more than that, *Feng.*"

Wind. He knows she's trying to be gentle. She calls him that in quiet times, when she clings to him. And now what he had not wanted to see becomes clear.

"I'm not blind," he says, although that's exactly what he's been. "I've seen you with him. It isn't so hard to figure out what he is to you. But I don't understand why. Why would you do this to us?"

"I'm sorry," she says. "But I have to."

"Just come with me to see the house."

"I'm sorry."

He stands in an autumn shadow, the new house looming behind him. The brick wall that surrounds the garden reminds him of the walled courtyard of the old houses in China, the kind that are now mostly gone. In the corner, in a tangle of ivy, is a mossy bench. He brushes away leaves and acorns, and sits. It is the kind of garden his father would have loved, where he could grow vegetables as in those long ago days. He might have built a small pond, a waterfall. Fengqi pictures a birdfeeder in the shape of a pagoda. His father could sit on the bench and watch colorful carp in the pond, visited by finches and sparrows, and allow himself to be transported to a time before everything changed, before the sea rose and covered the earth, before the wars, before flying here into the nothingness that his life became.

There is room enough in this house for the boys, for Claudia if she will come to help, for Maddie's mother when she chooses to visit. And there is more than enough room for the ghost of Maddie herself, and his father, and all of his ancestors, wherever they are.

2011 Prime Mincer Poetry Prize Winner

"A poem that brings language, imagination, and great heart. It has a primal energy about it."

-Rodney Jones

Nancy Cook

Aran Island Knit

This is the story that's told:
a fisherman's sweater is
like a dog tag knit in code,
the zig zags, baskets, diamonds
a pattern to be read.
Every family has its own that
each might know its own. Might

know when the sea in the devil's hands
yanks the face and soul from a body
and that body, broken, now in care
of angels, is gently handed back
to shore; they'll know, the women,
whose name to carve in limestone.
Arm in arm, they'll pray

for the repose of him whose clan
is written in the language of
the stitching.   A myth it is, or a lie,
to benefit the tourist trade, for the
fancy of the outside world who see us
quaint, a tragic people, romance
in our fatalistic charm. When

what's real is that Callum's gone.
Off to find work in Dublin or Galway
or, God forbid, Liverpool. No life
for one whose soul since birth has been
surrounded by the Gaelic sea, whipped
by the storytelling winds of Celtic skies.
What will save him from the devil's myths
bandied about by men, lads who
follow like sheep, telling tales of
tales plaited in wool? They are not our
stories, which are stories of truth,
which are woven in the passing clouds,
random cables and airy honeycombs,
simple joys not meant to last;

which are woven in the dark and dank
seaweed, twisted and spongy, the smell
of ancient life and everpresent death
strongly mingled. And when Callum
returns, if he returns, his soul yanked,
his face changed by distant storms, then,
how will I know it is he?

Deshler, in August

i

Germans settled this land. Farmers,
pick and hoe men and wives. Solid folk who,
like their parents before them, and theirs before that,
marked the seasons with their plows,
measured fortunes in canning jars and futures
in names scrawled into family Bibles.
In acre upon acre of neat rows, dug deep
and endlessly straight, their legacy endures,
the prospering fields a tangible
affirmation of the ancestral values
of clarity, and constancy, and certainty.

Every year it's celebrated,
this land and its traditions. Under heavy
canvas, old folkways are revived and
more or less remembered, as August heat
rises to the ceiling and then, finding
no window of escape, settles like a hot fog
on the tent floor. Every year, Fritz Krohnberg
·does his yodels, and every year, without fail,
Herr Becker calls the polkas. Old men
in burnished lederhosen
tend the wooden kegs. The women
draw sausages dripping with oils
from steaming pots and ladle warm, vinegary
potato salad from sweaty vats. Children,
shifting their weight from one bare leg to another

and scratching at mosquito-bitten arms,
wait impatiently for samplings of strudel
lathered in cream whipped thick as butter.

It's like it's always been, a tableau
as predictable as sweltering, torpid
August itself, a pattern so familiar,
it requires no blueprint to plot it out.

                    ii
But Jo Koestler says things have changed.
Imagine, she says, the Lutheran Church
has air conditioning. Two fast food restaurants
in town and parking meters on the square.
There's talk of townhomes being built
over by the warehouse, low cost housing
for the migrants who drift in like robins
from south Florida every spring.
It's controversial business, not spoken of with favor;
but the State's got the people nervous,
building pressure to raze the summer shacks,
provide hot water and electric heat. Downtown
may look different, but it's what's happening on
the farms, the change that can't be measured,
that gives the locals a feeling
of being unsettled. Jo loves this town,
this flat and open country. But she will miss
this summer's fest, she and Bud, first time
in thirty-some-odd years.

                    iii
Last night, inside the big tent,
children of the farm workers -- the del Gados
and the Diaz boys and Ana Marquez —
grew restless as the music of
accordions and clarinets played.

Ana, whose parents left the fields,
bought the old Schmitt place on the corner of Elm,
and opened up a grocery, eased to the platform
in the center of the tent and, with back arched,
held a slim arm out to Ricky Diaz in a
bold invitation to join her. The del Gados
and the other Diaz brothers followed,
and soon the cast of youthful celebrants
held the dance floor with their spinning
as if it were their stage. Under the town's
blue-eyed gaze they danced, these dark children,
flashing red and black, heels like castanets.
They did not dance the polka.

                    iv
Bud Koestler's had a stroke. Happened
at the plant, three weeks past, minutes
before the 5:10 whistle telegraphed
the change of shifts. A seizure, without
warning, like a passing freight train,
the foreman said. Bud's legs got trapped
like insects underneath the factory's
obsolete machinery. He's home now
from the hospital, but can't do much:
legs won't budge, fingers tremble,
his hearing's weak. So every day he sits,
wheel chair against the window, he sits
and stares at distant roads, visible
through the curtain split.
Doctors have their ways, says Jo.
She has faith in them. And in the Lord.
Insurance, it don't cover near enough,
she says. She prays for better times.

v

The corn has reached full height.
Crisp, dry stalks rustle in the
faint breeze; they crowd the landscape
with their tight, neat rows, parting
scarcely wide enough for
the railway to channel through.
Standing on the trestle, you can see where
the divided tracks meet to make a point,
somewhere up north. The seven fifty-five's
been by, leaving in its wake
a red steam that burns into the flatness.
Horizons made for thinking:
what is possible is endless,
and what is endless, possible.

Penny Stock Guy

In the morning, I went downstairs and opened the living room curtains. A man with snowy white hair was sitting in a lawn chair in my driveway. I stood there a few minutes, slipped on my shoes, and headed outside. My first thought was I'd forgotten to make my car payments, and this was some sneaky new stunt by the car repo guys. Or maybe he was here for the dryer, which I'd bought on an installment plan. I got closer, and the man took on shape, contour, and size. He became my next-door neighbor's father, Howie Coleman, Bob's father. In red plaid pajamas and an eggshell blue robe.

I almost asked if he was all right, but stopped myself. Howie was eighty, but could easily pass for sixty. He was built like a bull. Full head of hair, strong shoulders, and a chiseled chest—I saw him swimming in Bob's new pool every day, hurtling himself in, slapping his big hands in an aggressive crawl stroke, then hoisting himself up and out. Dripping wet, he pumped out a rapid fifty, sixty push-ups by the side of the pool, then flipped on his back for a set of sit-ups. Impressive. We'd had a handful of exchanges, heated and otherwise, over the fence, mostly me asking if he'd turn down the disco music at his pool party.

"Hello Howie."

"Heard you just retired," grinned Howie. "Got two words for you: retirement kills."

"Why are you sitting in my driveway?"

The top buttons of Howie's pajama shirt were undone, revealing a thatch of white, curly chest hair. "Waiting to have a word. Every morning you come out at the same time and pick up your newspaper. Like goddamn clockwork. You'd be easy to pick off if I were a hit man."

He reminded me of one, or a wanna-be. Same swagger, word choice, the way he peeled out of the driveway in his black Thunderbird with darkened windows, tires wildly squealing. Once he rode my bumper driving home, pulled into his driveway, leaped out of his car, and shouted, "Granny!" Now he had my newspaper tucked under his arm. I'd hinted once it would help if he invited me to one of his pool parties. No invitation yet. The ratio was usually ten women to one man. I guessed Howie liked it that way.

"If you don't do something, you're a goner," he said. "I've lived this long by a bunch of this and that, but lately by the fun and games of day trading."

It took me months to make up my mind to retire. For three decades I'd taught English at the local community college. When there was enough interest, my subject was poetry, with a special emphasis on the Romantics. My secret love. Keats, Byron, Coleridge, don't get me started. I hadn't taught poetry in years, nor had I seen the students clamoring for it any time soon. So at age sixty four, I retired.

"You need to get in on the action," said Howie. "Join the big boys."

My pension was laughable, I said. My pea-size savings were in a CD, which rolled over at a measly two percent year after year. The world of money had never interested me. I'd tried reading Adam Smith's *The Wealth of Nations* and Keynesian theory and supply-side economics, but my eyes always glazed over. I was mildly ashamed of this. Most men my age had at least a working knowledge of bonds and interest rate fluctuations.

"We're talking penny stocks." Howie lit up a cigarette. "Nickels and dimes. Then I do my rough magic and turn them into dollars and more dollars." He'd made enough to bring himself life, liberty, and a large quantity of happiness.

Which I'd seen from my backyard—kegs, bottles of wine, piles of food. And just at that moment, I remembered the psychologist's marshmallow experiment. If a kid gobbled up the marshmallow instead of holding out to earn two, it turns out the kid was more likely to be a drop-out, an addict, or a hoodlum. Howie seemed the type to devour his right away then ask for more. "I'm also no stranger to risk," he said. "I used to partake in a serious 24-7 poker game at Restful Haven."

Here, finally, was common ground. "My girlfriend lives out there," I said.

"What's her name?"

"Alva Lemon."

Yellow leaves floated down from the birch and onto the driveway.

"Sure. Alva. Good-looking."

Alva had a thin figure, pale blue eyes, a face that still held a gleam of beauty, a carefully groomed look of matching pants and suit coats. She was full of spunk and vitality and chose to live at the Restful Haven not for health reasons but for its lively social calendar. If she wanted, she could take a class—art, exercise, literature—any hour of the day.

"Older women. They're an overlooked lot," said Howie, flicking ash on my driveway. "An untapped well of pent-up sexual energy."

I could have guessed Howie's view. At his pool parties, Mr. Appetite for Life was always reaching for hugs, grabbing some woman with coiffed white hair and smooching her cheek, then whisking her off to a corner. From my upstairs study window, I had a good view of things.

"She's quite a lady," I said.

"What are you talking about? She's a fox! Has she mentioned marriage?"

"I've been lukewarm." I felt the old showing-off instinct kicking in. "I'm a Sunday-only guy. Just Sundays. Don't want her to think she's got me wrapped around her finger."

Last semester I'd been under a lot of pressure—teaching four classes, in addition to remedial English for the growing number of illiterate freshman, and serving on the Committee to Improve Committees. In actuality, I didn't have time. But now what was my excuse?

"Don't let her talk you into marriage. It comes with a lot of wild-ass expectations. Tried it three times."

I was flattered by Howie's willingness to step out of his house wearing his pajamas at 7:00 a.m. in forty nine degree weather, just to proposition me like this. Salt of the earth types never talked to me. I knew nothing about machines or fixing lawn mowers or baseball teams. Frankly, since I'd retired I couldn't remember having a conversation this long during the weekday. Unlike my former colleagues who peppered their conversations with polysyllabic words and modifying clauses and phrases until it was unclear what anyone was talking about, Howie was a straight-shooter. How refreshing.

I told him to come over in a half hour and we'd discuss it. Of course he'd personally gain from whatever he was up to, but I saw nothing wrong with that. He came back dressed in a silver tracksuit, looking like a shark. He stopped in the entrance of my house, as if assessing whether the place was safe.

Suddenly I saw it through someone else's eyes: my overreliance on burnt orange furniture—a two-seater couch, two chairs, a rug. A dusty macramé on the wall. Twenty years ago, after my divorce, I'd bought the house, which came with the furniture. I'd always planned on redecorating, but the years drifted by and here I was, an island surrounded by burnt orange furniture.

"We'll get you fixed up, Cliffy, boy. In no time, you'll have enough money to chuck this crap. Liven things up."

We sat on the couch and Howie turned on his laptop. He logged into ETrade and showed me his portfolio. I didn't know what I was looking at—a lot of acronyms, ATC, NHTY, BOC. The most important thing was the number at the bottom, he said. As a whole, his investments had gone up 17 percent.

"Here's how it works: any stock I recommend and you invest in, I charge a small fee. No big deal. It does well, another small percentage."

Something came to mind. Last semester I had a kid from Cairo who'd headed home to help run a family business called EE1!!. Howie looked it up. EE1!! specialized in digging ditches and building bridges and was selling for one and a half cents a share.

"You could get in right now."

I didn't know. While the first two weeks of retirement had been enjoyable, lolling in bed, reading the newspaper for hours, and riding my bike around the neighborhood, I'd begun to wonder: had I made the right decision? Sleep was fitful. I jerked awake, covered in sweat, heart pounding, thinking I had to be somewhere and it was very late. I missed my job. Was it really so bad, the backstabbing and fights over pitifully small territories of knowledge—who would get to teach what? Because I couldn't imagine how I'd spend the rest of my days.

I reminded Howie I didn't have a lot of savings.

"Oh, come on. Why don't you live for once?"

Howie gave me an assignment. I'd hunt for hot stocks by rooting around the academic stuff—reading newspapers, magazines, dusty books. Howie would do what he did best: he'd loiter in cafes, diners, the five-and-dime, the bowling alley, the hardware store, the drug stores, the ice cream shop. He'd prowl the neighborhood for trends, gossip, gestures, and innuendo. He'd skulk around in grocery stores. For this he'd needed a small expense account.

"Why?"

Howie shifted in his chair, and his tracksuit glistened. "Can't loiter without dropping some coins. Security gets antsy."

We shook hands. Howie's palm was dry and cracked and his knuckles huge, as if each of his fingers had been broken. He handed me back my newspaper and left. As soon as the door closed, panic seized me. What had I done? Why did I feel I was in business with a small-time crook?

Sunday morning, I got into my car and drove out to Restful Haven in Pacifica, with its rows and rows of 1950s houses. Cape Cods, they were called, with steep roofs, chimneys and two windows peering out at a 180 degree view of the Pacific Ocean.

Except Restful Haven wasn't up on the hill, but down in the valley. You couldn't see a thing except the highway. And only when the traffic slowed down could you hear the waves beat against the shore.

I pulled into a visitor's spot, and as I strolled out back to the miniature golf course, where I usually found Alva, I called Howie and told him to buy one hundred dollars of EE1!!.

"You're in the game now!" he said.

Alva waved at me. She was dressed in a short red golf skirt that showed off her nice legs. I thought of a line from a Coleridge poem: "Fear that—the spark self-kindled from within." She was playing with a woman who resembled a huge cotton ball, and a tall man with enormous ears.

"What's your handicap?" said Alva.

"Bad knees."

She laughed and squeezed my arm. I gave her a peck on the cheek.

Three months ago, I met Alva in the parking lot of a massive department store. She was attempting to roll a shopping cart full of plastic organizing bins to her car. After I loaded up her car, I invited her to coffee and a danish. We'd both grown up in Washington state, we discovered, not far from Ander's Apple Farm. Her favorite ice cream was vanilla. As was mine. Moved by the beautiful music of her laughter, I surprised myself by asking if I might see her again. "Why, that would be lovely," she said, her round cheeks blushing.

Alva squared up her hips and sent her ball within an inch of the hole. The man went next and hit a decent shot. Cottonball landed near a windmill.

"OK, Clifford, make me proud," said Alva.

My ball bounced off the cement boundary and dribbled into the moat, scaring off a bunch of pigeons.

The man said to keep my head down. "You got to focus."

"Right."

"You got to want it. Be here."

"Right."

"Oh, we're just having fun here," said Alva. "Someone will win, someone will lose. Who cares?"

The pigeons flew back onto the course and strutted. Alva got a big laugh out of that. We played a couple more holes. "I just need to practice," I said. Immediately, I knew what she'd say. She'd been hinting at it ever since I retired.

"You can come out here any day of the week now," she said sweetly, "and practice with me."

"Got something." Howie shoved his hands into the pockets of his tracksuit.

"How many of those outfits do you have?"

"Five. On sale. Waiting for the next sale and I'll buy five more. When I find something I love, I go after it."

We were standing outside on my front porch. I'd found him there at six thirty, when I opened the door to get the newspaper. Clouds of steam puffed out of our mouths. The sun was trying to come out, but was losing to the heavy fog. Howie followed me inside to debrief me. For two days, he'd staked out Grinwald's Grocery Store. He shook his head, looking amazed. "Here's the word: soup. Soup is flying off the shelf. Everyone's buying it, hoarding it, devouring it. Don't ask me why. The why doesn't matter. It's the what and the how and the who and the when."

"What brand?"

"Doesn't matter. It's all flying. Chicken noodle, mushroom, gumbo. People are eating it up."

"Don't I need a name if I'm going to invest?"

"I'll give you a name. TSC."

"Never heard of it."

"New guy on the block. Cheapest on the shelf. Made in Taiwan. They must use six-year-olds to make this stuff because a can costs thirty cents. The stock's going for two cents a share."

I felt dubious. "I need to move slowly on this."

"Don't be a chicken shit."

The last time someone called me that to my face was fourth grade. I'd refused to slide down a grassy hill on a piece of flimsy cardboard. I saw myself flying off, tumbling down the hill, breaking all my bones, having to wear a full body cast for the rest of my grade school years. It just didn't seem worth it.

"I'm putting in $250," Howie winked. "That's how the big boys play."

"Good for you."

I watched him do the trade. So simple. Push a couple buttons, $250 becomes ten million shares. Howie picked up a stale bagel from my table, as if he was thinking of eating it, then tossed it on a plate where it landed with a loud thud. "You owe me fifty dollars. I had to buy some things at the grocery store."

"Hey, I'm not investing."

"You will." His voice, a gruff tenor, didn't invite dissent.

EE1!!. had just dropped from a dollar to sixty-three cents.

"Uh-oh. Trouble in Cairo." Howie smiled, as if enjoying the fact that I'd lost money.

"Oh, come on. I'm sure it'll bounce back."

"Don't count on it. In the Middle East, things can go from good to worse in a second. I know. Saw the pyramids. Rode a camel. By the way, how's my gal Alva?"

"Great." I told him we played golf yesterday.

"She's a helluva good golfer. She used to scorch me."

"You've played golf with her?"

"Hell, I used to date her. She's a hottie. I also once owned a gun."

After Howie left, I tried to calm down by reading Keats. When that didn't help, I picked up Keynes's *General Theory of Employment, Interest and Money* and kept at it for an hour. Basically the government spends money to liven up the economy. As a life-long Democrat, I'd thoroughly enjoyed the Johnson administration, with his Great Society Program. So this theory appealed to me greatly. Why couldn't it have the same effects when put to work in a man's life?

I got up and paced the living room, trying to decide. Should I sell EE1!!? I went out on the back porch. It looked like someone had torn up a bunch of clouds and thrown them around. What could Alva possibly see in a guy like Howie? She'd always complimented me on my good manners, my proper use of the English language, how I waited a month before I kissed her.

This guy probably jumped her bones the first date. The marshmallow phenomenon. Going back inside, I called Howie on his cell phone. Said to sell half my holdings in EE1!!. What did I know about Cairo?

"Good thinking." He was in the car and as soon as he got home, he'd do the trade. In a proud voice, he told me TSC had gone up 35 percent. "You missed the big jump."

I told him, Buy a hundred dollars.

"Get ready to make some real dough."

Feeling ebullient, I took everything out of the refrigerator and scrubbed it with water and vinegar. When I was done, it sparkled and smelled halfway decent in there. Then I called Alva. "I wanted to hear your sweet voice."

She laughed. She was playing wiffle ball with a group of

friends, including a man named Howie. He said he knew me.

I tried to laugh, too. "I was thinking of coming by later." I blinked, startled at myself. "I'll take you out to dinner."

A pause. "But you said Mondays were out. You were too busy. I'm sorry, Clifford, I've made plans."

I didn't ask. In the background I heard Howie's great big voice bragging how he was the only one with balls in this game.

How about tomorrow night?

"Tuesday?" I heard the hint of alarm in her voice. "But we never—I'm sorry—" She had an opening Friday.

When I got off the phone, something cold gusted inside me. I threw on my coat and headed out to the newspaper stand at the corner deli. It was run by a middle-aged man from Saudi Arabia who argued with the radio. "It's not going to fucking rain!" he shouted as I came into the store. He kept a large selection of reading material so he could stay current not only with the weather, but with Middle Eastern and European affairs. I bought a stack, went home, and plopped down on the couch.

All afternoon, I read about China, Singapore, Germany, India, Egypt, the United States, Cuba. I scoured New York's entertainment scene, Buenos Aires's, Tokyo's. Frantic for an investment opportunity, I was seized with the idea of making a whole lot of money fast. I found something. A new restaurant in downtown San Francisco, near Union Street. Recently opened, it held live martial arts demonstrations in the lobby and had a pond with swans and trees with golden-faced saki monkeys. On the second floor, they had plans for ballroom dancing or bingo or belly dancing. Szechuan Palace had just been listed on the penny stock exchange.

Any other time, I'd have slept on it. Maybe talked it over with Ira Frasner who taught economics at the college. Any other time, the mishmash of pipe dreams would have sounded suspect, but now I logged on, figured out how to access my portfolio and bought three hundred dollars of Szechuan Palace. Proud owner of fifteen million shares, I instantly became the majority owner.

I wanted to call Alva and boast about it. I wanted to hear her congratulate me, say I'd made a smart move. Instead I called the restaurant and made a reservation for Friday. I told him who I was.

"We have big plans," said the man on the phone. "A boxing ring in lobby, crickets in cages in bathrooms. Bring good luck. You come by, we give you cricket for good luck. For being major owner." They'd give me the best seat in the house, he said, only charge me half price. Free white rice.

Howie pulled out a notebook from his tracksuit pant pocket. "Live deer."

We were in the living room. I had removed the plates of stale food and tried to scrub the stains off the table. Earlier this morning, I'd imagined inviting Alva over and cooking an elaborate seven-course dinner. I heard us talking and laughing, carrying on into the wee hours of night. So late, she'd decide to stay over. I found myself anxiously vacuuming and fluffing pillows.

"People are buying deer. Putting them in the woods near their houses to create a sense of nature."

"Where'd you hear this?"

He chuckled. "Cliffy, boy. You never know what you'll pick up. I'm out in the field, see, checking things out, surveying the candy store. Two women start jabbering about live deer. They'd put in an order for two."

It sounded suspicious, but what did I know about investing? And TSC was up 60 percent.

This time Howie had imported his own breakfast—coffee and a plastic bag of dry Honey O's. He reached in and popped a handful into his mouth.

"I found a company that's producing enhanced water," I told him. "Based in Shanghai."

"That's the dumbest thing I've ever heard. Enhanced water? By the way, you still owe me for TSC."

I wrote out a check. Howie let his eyes flick over it before pocketing it.

"So you played wiffle ball with Alva." I cocked my head nonchalantly.

Howie stopped chewing and held up one hand right in front of my face, like he was thinking of smothering me. "I don't mix business and pleasure. You want to step outside the office, we can talk pleasure. In the office, I talk business."

I brushed some lint off my pants. "I'm not sure, but I think we got off on the wrong foot here. I mean, I'm seeing Alva."

Standing, Howie headed outside to the back porch. I followed. "You mentioned her name. We always had a good time together. So I drove out there. Big deal." Howie dumped the rest of the Honey O's into his mouth. "Do you want the name of the deer company or not?"

On Friday, I took Alva to Szechuan Palace. In the lobby, two squat Chinese men in white pants and coats were kicking each other's thick thighs. Each kick elicited a grunt or a quick inhale of pain.

"Welcome, Lawrence," said the general manager.

"The name is Clifford."

The general manager pointed to the two men. "Top karate experts. They fight. People eat, come out and see fight, eat some more. Fighting makes people hungry."

Alva and I got the grand tour: the swan pond, which included a swarm of black gnats hovering above brackish water, a glassed-off area with monkeys hanging from fake pine trees, and three thousand square feet upstairs, which was plywood and dust and loose nails.

"Big plans," the general manager kept saying.

I forced a bright smile. "Have you ever run a restaurant before?"

Yo-Po said in Shanghai he had been head waiter. He'd learned a lot there. And he got to eat for free.

I ordered up a feast: potstickers, wonton soup, General Tso's chicken, Kung Pao shrimp, Mongolian beef, bok choy, white rice, jasmine rice, lychee sorbet. Was I trying to impress Alva or Yo-Po?

"Heavens, Clifford." Alva took out a bottle of pills, shook one out, and popped it into her mouth.

"Don't worry. We'll take home what we don't eat."

She smiled. "So here we are on a Friday."

"I guess I don't always see what's right in front of me. I apologize for that."

Alva smiled. I reached over and held her hand. I looked around. Second week in business. The place was half full.

"It's new," she said. "It'll catch on. Though I have to say, it's a bit frightening having all those monkeys staring at you."

Ten monkeys were hanging from trees, watching us eat. Except one, who was scampering around the cage, sneakily gathering up all the bananas and stuffing them into a hole in a tree, as if hoarding them for later. Were they not fed properly? I'd have to talk to Yo-Po about it.

"So how was Howie?"

The waiter brought the soup and pot stickers. Alva nibbled, but I was surprisingly ravenous.

"Oh, he's Howie. No one makes me laugh like Howie."

I could see that. Howie was one big parody of something. A gangster, a gambler, a down-on-his-luck ladies'man.

The food was greasy. It left you feeling fuller than you should be, wanting to walk for several hours, concerned about your poor heart.

As we put on our coats, Yo-Po handed me a cricket. A thin brown bug in a bamboo cage. "Good luck for you."

We walked around Union Square. The night was bright with street lamps and lit up window displays. So many gadgets and doo-dads. Mr. Live for Today probably saw investment opportunities galore when he strolled by these windows.

"So are you seeing funny Howie now, too?"

She squeezed my hand. "He mentioned something. Since you're only a Sunday guy, he said, I must have a lot of time on my hands."

What was next? A marriage proposal?

"I'm going to go out on a limb here." I took both of Alva's hands in mine. "If you agree, I'd like to make Fridays a standing date between us."

She smiled. "Fine. Howie said if he didn't see me on Mondays and Wednesdays, he'd just die."

"Oh, he'd die, would he?"

"You know how he is," she said. "He pretended to have a heart attack right in front of me until I agreed. He had me in stitches laughing."

We'd made it back to my car, which was parked in front of Szechuan Palace. We got in, I turned on the heater and the cricket began to chirp. Through the front window in the fluorescent lit lobby we could see the two men still fighting, sweat dripping off their faces, which were beet red.

Tuesday morning, I showered, then drove to Clement Street and picked up flowers, chocolates. I was reaching for some glazed donuts, when a woman with rings on all her fingers grabbed them before me. "Sorry. My son loves these." She rushed toward the check-out stand, as if I might tackle her.

As I drove, I whistled along with the radio, *Let the Good Times Roll*. Why didn't I do this long ago? Just surprise her. Show up on one of our off days? People enjoy the element of surprise, to a point. It wakes them from their deep slumber. I ate one of the donuts and powder sprinkled on my pants. Really, I should be thankful to Howie for finally getting me off my butt.

Alva was in the community center room, doing yoga to a DVD. Cottonball was there, as were Mr. Know-It-All-Golfer and Howie. All of them on the floor, their legs straight out in front of them.

"What a surprise," said Alva.

"Mr. Sunday himself," said Howie.

"Funny finding you here," I told him.

"I was about to say the same thing to you."

"Why don't you join us, Clifford?" said Alva.

I put the box of donuts on the table and sat on her other side as she reached for her toes.

"We've added in Fridays," I said.

"Wow. Big move."

"Breathe deeply," said the woman on the DVD. "Open your chest and let the air flow."

"Hey, Cliffy, boy. Watch this." Howie did a headstand, then rolled out of it and with his belly facing the ceiling, turned himself into a bridge.

His curly hair touched the floor.

"Shh," said Alva, pointing to the DVD.

"What do you got?" said Howie.

I pushed a mat up against the wall and kicked up. Blood bounded into my brain and the world went dizzy.

"You need a wall. Pussy."

"Please," said Mr. Know-It-All.

"Pipe down, asshole," said Howie.

On the DVD the woman said something about the spine releasing. I counted to thirty, thinking of a friend of mine. He attributed his good health to headstands. Blood left my heart, pooled in my head. I wasn't about to say anything, but I felt a sharp pain in my back.

"That's nothing," said Howie.

"Oh, I've got something" I crumpled to the mat.

"Whatever you've got, I've already got it beaten."

"Yeah?"

"Can you do this?" He put one leg over his neck in a yogic position.

Mr. Know-It-All said, "How about I just get a bat and you two go at it?"

Howie got up and ate four donuts.

"Alva, are you lapping this up?" said Cottonball, giggling.

Alva smiled and clapped her hands. "OK, boys, how about breakfast?"

"Can I have a word with you?"

We stepped outside. Acorns covered my deck, making it difficult to stand. I gripped the railing and turned to Howie. "What's going on? You? Alva?"

"Oh, Alva and I are just having a little fun." He gave me a punch to the shoulder. "A beautiful woman nearing the big curtain. She needs to be courted and wooed, she needs to laugh and remember life is good, even if it isn't."

I reminded him I'd added Fridays.

Howie rolled his eyes and spit.

Why was I sitting here listening to Mr. Live It Up? "I'm going at my own pace."

"You better pick it up or you're going to lose her. Remember, I know how to woo the women. And I was once her number one."

"I won't be threatened," I said.

In an instant, Howie had me in a headlock. I tried to elbow his stomach, but he only laughed and gave me a noogie. I tried to kick his shin, but just swiped his ankle. "Look at us," said Howie, "over a woman. Now you're in the game, Cliffy."

Finally Howie let go.

"I think our arrangement is over," I told him.

"Oh, come on. I've made you real money."

Szechuan Palace was down 50 percent, and Yo Po kept leaving frantic messages on my machine about needing more funding. EE1!! had declared bankruptcy. My trading days were numbered—I didn't have a knack for it, and my blood pressure was sky-high. I'd already left messages with the dean, asking if he needed an instructor. I'd offered to head up two thankless jobs—the chess team, and the English Department's Committee to Improve the Department.

"Making the big play for love." Howie patted me on the back. "No hard feelings, but I'll give you a run for your money. Which won't be hard because you don't have much money."

The afternoon felt big and empty. Back inside my house, Howie put on his shark coat. "Pretty fucking quiet in here." He pointed to the cricket cage, at the bottom of which the brown cricket lay on its side, its six legs stiff. "Good luck. You're going to need it."

The leaves turned red and orange, and the light autumnal and golden, with its promise of frigid air. On Fridays, I took Alva to Mimi's Dance Parlor and held her tight, twirling her under the disco ball until her cheeks flushed rosy. I asked Alva for Tuesday and Thursday and when she agreed, my sorry golf game improved slightly.

Through my living room window, I watched Howie roar out of his driveway in his Thunderbird, knowing full well where he was going because he wasn't wearing his shark tracksuit, but trousers, a red scarf, and a tight button-down shirt that showed off his big chest. I'd sigh, counting the hours until I could safely drive out, without colliding into Howie and ending up in another yoga showdown.

I began teaching poetry at the university. I memorized lines and recited them to Alva over dinner in the Restful Haven cafeteria. She and her friends gathered around to hear me quote

Keats and Shelley and the others. All of this deliberate, to set me miles apart from Howie. Though I couldn't tell if the edge was real.

It was during one of these performances that Mr. Big Shot sauntered in. Dressed in a dark brown three-quarter coat with a matching hat and a snazzy pair of cowboy boots. His gait slowed when he saw me, but he quickly recovered himself and charged over to the table. He pulled up a chair next to Alva. I had been reciting Keats's *Bright Star.*

"Go ahead," he said, picking up a toothpick, "don't let me interrupt."

I hesitated.

Alva reached across the table and touched my knuckle. One of the blue-haired women nodded and smiled at me, then adjusted her hearing aid.

"Hey, sugar pops," Howie said to Alva. He took out the toothpick and gave her a kiss right on the lips. Reaching inside his coat, he pulled out a large box of chocolates and set it on the table in front of her.

Why was he sitting next to her and me across the table? "'To feel forever its soft fall and swell—'"

Howie spat out the toothpick and laughed loudly. "Poetry. Sissy stuff."

My face turned red hot. "Straight from Mr. High Finance himself."

"Got that right."

"Nickel and diming your way through the world, are you?"

"Better than earning zippo, nada, the big zero."

This hustler was trying to win over Alva. Alva deserved better. I deserved better, though I wasn't sure what I meant by that. "A pathetic penny stock guy."

"What did you say, pal?"

His face turned furiously pale like creamed wheat.

"You're just a pathetic two-bit wheeler dealer." I grabbed a dinner bun and threw it at his head. Someone gasped. I reached for the nearest thing—red jello with a dab of whip cream—and flung it. It dribbled down the front of his silk shirt. Satisfaction washed through me like a wave. He snatched a brussel sprout from Alva's plate. It bounced off my chin. I threw the sprout back, hitting his ear.

"For heaven's sake!" said Alva.

Howie's brows joined together like the hilt of a sword. He ripped the cellophane off the box of chocolates and threw one at me. Rage welled up in me. I grabbed two and fired back. It felt like I'd been waiting for this moment, storing up for it.

"You son of a bitch," he growled.

"Boys!"

"Can't take your own medicine?" I said.

Howie's face glistened. His nose looked like a white bulb. Loose skin hung from his throat, like a wattle of an ugly, old bird.

"I can take anything, puff ball."

I picked up a glass of water and was going to throw it in his face, but someone seized my arm. The same beefy security guy who had Howie by the arm. "Out. Both of you. Out."

"I'll show myself to the door," said Howie, yanking his arm away. He stalked down the hall to the front door.

"What about you, buddy?" said the security guy. "Think you can handle showing yourself out? You have to be a big boy, you know."

I sent flowers. Cards of apology. *I am mortified by my behavior. If you can forgive me—I'd love to see you.* I thought about quoting a line of poetry, but decided to let it rest.

A week later, Alva called and invited me over for a Sunday golf game. I thought I'd find her on the golf course, but she was in her room, still in bed, in a white nightgown with small pink roses.

"Are you feeling all right?"

Her new glasses kept drifting down the bridge of her nose.

"I feel dizzy," she said, her words coming slowly. She looked pale, slightly dazed. "I can't remember where the bathroom is."

I went to find a doctor.

The nurse took her temperature, blood pressure and pulse, then called an ambulance. In my car, following, I gripped the steering wheel and made a plea to no one in particular: Please don't let anything happen to her. Please. When was the last time I prayed? Someone help me.

"You'll be all right." I sat next to Alva's hospital bed and held her hand. She closed her eyes, and I leaned over and kissed her cheek, then her throat. I could feel her pulse in my lips.

She'd had a stroke. Her speech was slowed, perhaps permanently. She'd have to take things slower.

When Alva returned to Restful Haven, Howie showed up a handful of times. I'd been avoiding him, but out my living room window, I saw him all decked out in one of his suits. I also saw him in his driveway with one of the beauticians from the Beauty Bar. I recognized her because I'd driven Alva there a couple times for a hair appointment. A gal with a thick middle who must have been the one to dye Howie's hair red.

Another time, Howie was with a large-boned woman with jet black hair. Where'd he meet this one? At his next pool party, he had both women on each arm, fawning all over him.

Howie waved at me over the fence. He looked tan and slightly younger with his red hair and his bathing suit covered with red hearts. "Hey, Cliffy, come on over. Have some fun." He gestured to the party and the steam billowing off the pool. I could see Bob bobbing around in there.

It seemed he'd put the food fight behind him. "Thanks," I said. "Another time."

I was on my way to see Alva. I was an everyday guy now, tending to the throb and beat of her heart. Howie said he was still trading—winning some, losing others, but overall, making enough and then some. "Not complaining, just living the good life."

We stood there a moment longer. "I'm sure she'd be happy to see you."

"Yeah."

"Can I say you'll stop by sometime?"

"Sure. Tell her that."

Though he didn't mean it.

I told Howie I was back to teaching.

"Suits you," he said.

Alva must be too quiet for him now, too subdued for his thrill-seeking heart. She liked to lie in bed for hours and listen to me read to her.

"You take good care of her," he said, punching me on the shoulder.

I used to feel like Howie had something on me. But when I stepped into Alva's room and she saw me, her face lit up and she gave me an ecstatic smile. Something caught in my throat. To see those pale blue eyes alert, sparkling again. She gestured to the chair.

I'd redecorated her room. She chose pale yellow paint for the walls, four prints of flowers and a bedspread of more flowers. It was like stretching out in a lush meadow of wild flowers. I put the new flowers in the vase, a big bouquet of yellow daisies.

"I saw Howie," I said, opening a book of Byron's poems.

"Oh? He really had a thing for me, didn't he?"

"He did."

"Boy, it made me feel special, having you two chase me like that. Imagine, at my age. Who'd have thought?" Taking out my handkerchief I wiped from her chin some egg from breakfast.

I wanted to say something nasty about Howie, but her eyes had misted. I'd never thought about it from her perspective. To be coveted, the golden one again, full of dazzle and bright light, for two men, not just one. How wonderful to feel so desired.

"He said to say hello," I said. "He hopes you're doing well."

"Oh, I'm glad. I hope they're no hard feelings."

"No," I smiled, "none at all."

Ocean View

A priest on the beach digs with a chrome shovel. Blue water shivers behind him. Jules, my kid sister, drowned when she was three. Whenever I float on my back I hear Jules calling my name. "Hoy," she goes, "Hoy Hoy!" She calls from a castle made of pearls under the sea. See that? The birthmark on my calf is expanding. A ladybug buzzes the window like a fly. Do I keep her in or release the luck? I slide the glass open. The blade of the shovel sticks in the sand. Better to have a beach full of luck than hog it for myself. Trouble—my glass mermaid arrives cracked in the mail. I am human, somewhere beyond repair.

Bald

That bald guy on the hill is yelling at his dog again. For what I don't know. Sometimes I hear him yelling at his wife and kids. Once he yelled at a sparrow. He's not a natural bald. On the contrary, I'm certain he shaves his crown at least twice a week because I've seen a five o'clock shadow when he patrols our fence. The shadow makes him look like a convict. I'll bet he'd go for the convict look if they'd let him get away with it at work. Being bald probably makes him feel tough. But he's not tough. He has a cream-puff belly and spindly arms like Tyrannosaurus Rex. I doubt he could fight his way out of a paper bag. He was barbecuing one Sunday when his wife joined him at the Weber Kettle—she cussed him, then lifted her leg like a dog and farted. That's the only time I ever heard him laugh.

Liechtenstein

The calf corpse appeared in the snow in the morning. The bull's fault, not mine, not its mama's, but this morning all that was left of that fault was a mound of tangled hair and a bit of untested hoof, a swell in a spot under snow. Its mama had gone on already to join the others. The living group's morning moan, their collective breakfast bellow, a stronger tug than what connects us to the dead.

My wife and I, our two kids (babies really) have been house-bound, snow-bound these last few weeks. What we have on our planet outside are sharply slicing, deeply furrowing January winds, and inside interminable loops of Elmo's Song, spliced with home-baked granola and diaper rash cream.

Kelly is standing in our one room that makes the living room and the kitchen, the baby in her arms and her tiny phone trapped between her ear and shoulder. In Los Angeles, her father is undergoing surgery. I think at all times of the cell phone makers, how they must not have had in mind a future where people held babies anymore. But then, we are a strange breed of children, living on a farm in the Midwest, swaddling our kids in cloth diapers and pureeing our homegrown apples into sauce while our parents in coastal metropoli drive cars nicer than ones we might even recognize as human modes of transport. Here we have Thomas the Tank Engine. A yellow toy front-loader. The three trucks in the barn like the three bears with their porridge, but all out of gas.

"What did she say exactly?" Kelly burps Gizmo. Similarly, her mother likes to be goaded before she explains things, in this case, what the doctor has said. We can get the wood stove in here crankin' and Kelly has taken off her tee-shirt. A squirt of what was once her own breast milk dribbles down her bare back.

"There's a big difference, Mom. A big difference." Kelly looks to me with her eyes and arms full, the phone and baby. I take them both.

"Is that you, Sparky?"

I do not mind this name because it has nothing to do with me personally but is only another kind of jab at Kelly. Mona explains that Kelly's dad will be kept overnight. She manages to imply that the doctors are just fastidious, like painters insistent on retouching the inside of a closet, billing by the hour.

But I can tell from how Kelly has begun in on the laundry (something for which neither of us has had, all the last week, the heart or stomach or other unknown, unnamed laundry organ to bear) that there is something more. Mona finally admits the doctors think there isn't much more they can do to prolong Kelly's father's life.

It's a phrase that makes me think of a taffy being pulled, something I wouldn't want to happen to my life, could it be spun out in sugar.

I did not marry my wife for her ability to do laundry, a thing I remind her of as she bemoans the piles that have grown from our hampers, that have metastasized to the mudroom, the pantry, the backs of the kitchen chairs, even the way-back of the van. Of course, a disregard for laundry is an easier ethic to espouse than to live with two babies in cloth diapers. The last two days while Gizmo has been having his way with my old YMCA T-shirts, Bonzo has run amok in his birthday suit, peeing in the plastic hatch of his John Deere tractor. It is a toy he rides slowly around the house with the self-import and exasperated patience of a mall cop on a Segway.

I begin to consider that my son has toilet trained himself to his tractor. Then I watch him put down Thomas the Tank Engine, board his green John Deere, and navigate the six feet to the ficus where he disembarks to poop into its ceramic pot. It is inevitable that sons will surpass their fathers.

"Do you want to go to L.A.?" I ask Kelly.

She is stuffing a washing machine with our clothes, low-ranking laundry, but I'm not the one on triage.

"Why did she talk him into it?" She asks the laundry. "Dad was happy to spend his next months however they came."

"He had months?"

"Well, no." She opens the cabinet where, as I know already, there is no soap. "You know, it was going to make him a new man. Give him fifty more years!" She puts a dryer sheet in the washing machine, closes the lid and turns the dial. Kelly's regard for Western medicine is like mine for Monsanto. And the Packers 2009 post-season loss to the Cardinals.

I realize I haven't told her about the calf.

"What?" she says. "What happened?"

By now she's stuffing a second load of our clothing into the wood stove, but I've already started and so I'll continue. The calf wasn't stillborn, but froze to death. Likely, it was its mother's licking, licking, licking in our recent sub-zero temperatures that accelerated its death.

And, let's not forget the bull. He was the first not to do his job in the right season of the year.

"Liechtenstein," Kelly says. "I never hear the word licking without thinking of it."

"The country?"

"One of the smallest in the world. The size of what anyone else would rightly call a city."

"But they've decided to call it a whole country."

We give Elmo the slow fade, a skill I learned DJing parties in college long before I could have foreseen its use in parenting. We've unfolded the living room couch into a bed and have collapsed here as a family, closer to the wood stove, further from the laundry piles. We pull up a Netflix, a strange European one with a lot of unruly pubic hair. In a few years, we won't be able to watch these kinds of movies, but now with only babies crawling over us we can. We can even get boners and, when the babies fall asleep, move ever so slowly to the far side of the sleeper. We make love absently and ardently, our organs at the first go missing each other entirely, jabbing at the dark.

I didn't have much of an idea of death when we first moved out here. I didn't see how it is about exactly half of farming. Or 100 percent, if you want to take the view that even to plant a seed is to put in motion the cycle that leads inevitably to its harvest. To your usurpation of its calories, until something comes along to usurp you.

Lately Bonzo has been into zerbits. He has these down, but not yet kisses, which elude him. His hugs are similarly sloppy. For as loving a kid as he's becoming, he cannot hug at all but only throw his arms around a victim's neck, the better for pinching with his surprisingly sharp, agile talons.

But it's crazy how complicated are these gestures, kiss, hug, how they require fine motor skill, precision, and so much experience with their receipt.

I walk around the house naked in the dark. We have no curtains, but no neighbors either. There are no streetlights and tonight (like last night) no visible moon. If I open the refrigerator door, its light floods the room, the yard, and stuns momentarily three acres of creeping, feeding nocturnal creatures.

I step over wooden blocks, Thomas the Tank Engine, and even the Barbies Kelly's twisted feminist (or maybe not?) sister bought her nephews for Christmas. I come to where Bonzo has parked his John Deere and know I will have to put a stop to this in the morning: this urine.

My own father was nearly killed twice in his life (that he knew of) and he liked to tell both stories (and with that punch line). Once was by his mother, birthing him. Shot me out across that room like a hockey puck! The second time he was shot was at a Seven Eleven during deer season, in what had appeared to be a hold up. He died finally of cancer, which led to our having this farm, this house.

I lean to kiss my boys on their sweating, sleeping heads. I think about how I will convince Kelly in the morning to buy a ticket. What I will have to say to trick her into believing I don't mind, that I can hold all this down alone.

And then, instead of giving Bonzo a kiss, I realize I am giving him a lick, a great slobbering one from his chin to his forehead.

I taste granola, diaper rash cream, urine.

Liechtenstein, I tell him, is a small, cold, beautiful country. We'll meet there again and again.

Cathy Kodra

The Trouble with Prayer

My aunt died on the floor from a chicken bone.
She died from a tiny bone that jabbed her intestine.
She died from a tiny bone, smaller than a passing thought,
which pierced her intestine. She died on the bathroom floor
scared and alone.

My aunt died in agony in a pool of bloody vomit.
She died in agony, vomiting blood, alone on the bathroom floor.
She died alone, crying out prayers, in agony and bloody vomit
on the bathroom floor. Did I remember to tell you that she was alone,
and she prayed? For weeks, she had mentioned pain, and she died
from a tiny bone in the body of a dead bird
that she ate while alone.

She said grace. I'm sure. She always said grace before
she ate. Alone or not, she prayed. She believed God
would cure her of the pain. My aunt believed God would take
away the pain and make her better. She told this to her neighbor
in the apartment upstairs after she swallowed a shred of chicken
embedded with the tiny piece of bone that she didn't even feel as it traveled
through her esophagus, into her stomach, and down to the small intestine,
which it quietly violated. The tiny sliver of bone sneakily slit the intestine and
then
lodged there, a bit in the way, and began to fester. This tiny, flexible piece of
bone
caused vomiting, pain, and death on the bathroom floor in my aunt's
downstairs apartment. No one heard her cries

no one heard her prayers. Apparently God was very busy
and didn't see why he needed to attend to this woman who gave
her entire adult life to his praise and contemplation. No one saved her.
She thought she had already been saved, years before. She thought if she prayed
her stomach would stop hurting, thought the sharp, terrible pains would cease.
She believed pain would cease.

As she said grace at the table that held the chicken that hid
the tiny bone that would stab her intestine and kill her, she prayed
herself into pain and agony. She said the words that would carry the shard
of bone, God's tiny arrow, to her ropey gut. She said the words that God
would hear, that would carry the sharp shiv of bone to her small intestine,
pierce it and find lodging there, later to be found by a tired forensic
pathologist who would remove the bone, which hardly looked like a bone
anymore, slimed black with bacteria, soft with sepsis, and place it
in a bag to be sent to the lab.

My aunt's prayer carried her proudly
to her grave. Thank you for this food, Oh Lord.
Bless this food in thy name, Oh Lord. Jesus Christ, Amen. He might
have been busy on another project, maybe making a new baby in some young
crack addict's womb. He might have been watching war news in Vietnam
and switched to The Price is Right just as she lay dying. He might have been
playing Bingo. To be fair, he might have been saving someone he deemed more
worthy. But for the grace of God, there go I! He didn't attend
to my aunt's prayer. He didn't cure her, or even take away
a smidgen of the pain. She could have cried Wolf! with better results. Skipped
grace, chewed more thoroughly. Gone to a medical doctor, witch doctor, acu-
puncturist, hypnotist, hands-on healer. Who knows

which part of her life he disavowed?

Donna Coffey

Talking to my Father at a Baby's Funeral

It's easy, he said,
to split an atom
but hard to fuse one.
Collide them in a mile-long tunnel,
they still won't stick.
Things want to fly apart.

Plancks, he said,
but I thought he said planks,
the logs in my red eyes,
the whitewashed boards
that line the baby's coffin
in the other room.

Plancks, he said,
are constant and infinitely small,
nearing zero but the energy escapes
and even scientists want to believe
in a fourth dimension
where lost things go,
like mass and babies.

Plancks.
There is no vacuum.
There are fields of light, oceans of light,
we swim in particles so tiny
they almost don't exist,
but they do.

But I knew what he saw
when he sank to the velvet kneeler.
He saw himself in a few years.
He saw what could have happened
to each of his own babies
and all the times he held it off.

In a photo of me when I was three
I am standing on a cliff
and his arm juts out in front of me
like a steel railing.

Not tender, never.
Our house a buttressed fortress.
Dad with a hammer, Dad with a drill,
Dad on the roof,
Dad buying two-by-fours at Hechingers.
Dad with stacks of boards
smelling fresh as a second chance.
Doors with deadbolts,
Talking to my Father at a Baby's Funeral Continued, no stanza
break

stairs with fat banisters,
the sturdy deck with boards
now splintered and raggedy,
nails sticking out,
beams sagging.

But he is telling me physics stories
at a funeral.
Still holding me
back from the edge.
Gripping me hard.

Mary Christine Delea

Needs More Science

The way I saw our cat Yowie, named for the Australian
aboriginal god
of the underworld, out of the corner of my eye for months
after he died, making him both dead and alive, like Schroedinger's
cat.

Pentimento.

Italians have such beautiful words; this one, the way an older
painting peeks
out from the painting we know:
Blue Boy and the mysterious dog.
Rembrandt's doubled hat brim in Flora.
The way Winslow Homer's seas will someday
become ponds: his walls, pebbles.

Stretched like a canvas, that word can mean
how your inner self, that child still in your psyche,
can crash through. Tired or anxious, the wrong thing said to or
about you,
and suddenly the eight-year-old you is there,
reacting for a moment, then sinking back
as the adult you, the now you, takes over.

And maybe that peek isn't always so bad, you a bit giggly at eight,
that age of infinity between ignorance and fear,
with your bangs and cotton playsuit, sitting next to your brother
on the Tilt-a-Wheel at Whalem Park, which unlike your child self

no longer exists, except as a ghost in old photographs and memories.

But there are other places, like Oaks Park, on the other coast,
where the carousel's center column still hums. The paintings
it exhibits, created first at the end of one world war and painted
over
years later as the world was again at war have sloughed off
their 1940's skins. Basic science with a magical result.

Like a containment field around childhood
pentimento has frayed the younger edges,
so a 1920s party girl in a red top and black shorts,
her limbs in movement to express joy,
now steps over mid-century cedars and junipers,
the trees part of a mostly peeled landscaped.
Pentimento continues in the way we can lose ourselves
on an amusement park ride—fugue state—no matter
how old we are. The way I remember
visiting Disneyland as a teen
but what I really remember
from that trip decades ago is my aunt making pasta
in her kitchen—I don't mean heating up water
and opening a box, but making the noodles
by hand. She and my uncle met in Italy at the end of the war
when she wasn't much older than I was then;
she'd seen enough of Mussolini's bad times
and was happy to leave. I had not been
through a war fought in my country, but life
already seemed tough. Even at sixteen how I longed to go back
to when I was eight and had no worries;
I longed to be on the Tilt-a-Whirl
with my brother, laughing, making sure my parents
waved each time we came around again,

which of course they did.
The way we whipped by—at eight

no one we knew had died, no one was
ghosting around in my peripheral view—
is always underneath everything.
And those rides, like that faded party girl
stepping over forests, keep us all spinning
even after the park has closed and been bulldozed,
its land turned into condos. That party girl
understands war, understands pentimento,
must know that science is against her, that one day she, too, will
fade away,
as if retreating into the underworld,
leaving nothing except canvas and smears.
But anyone who knows she is there
will always have her underneath,
under this world, like childhood, like a ghost cat, like innocence,
in the corner of the eye. Enternamente.

Carol V. Davis

John Bower, Biologist, Explains Bird Calls

The birds here on Sehome Hill differ from those
in Seattle, ninety miles south; a kind of dialect he says in a
voice so patient you'd think he was explaining the obvious.
Say the birds meet between the two cities, some would
mingle, a few might mate, though many females
would refuse the advances, despite coaxing.

Is it a kind of snobbery? The way my mother-in-law,
Boston-bred, looked down on the New Yorkers, as if
they'd just tumbled out of steerage, as her own parents had,
in fact, their leather suitcase shoved under the bunks,
squeezed shut with a rope that frayed all across the Atlantic.

The way she looked down on that New York accent,
be it tinged with a brogue or weighted down by a folksy Yiddish.
It's the difference between the snide call of a mockingbird and
the trill of a Townsend warbler: This one from the right side of the
tracks,
the mocker not. Even a mountain range can make a difference:
Remember the Valley girl accent everyone imitated in the 70s?

High up a bush tit nest hangs, its shape a sock,
brown, bits sticking out, either art or lack of attention to detail.
What will the birds eat? No salmonberries yet,
the coldest spring on record, though the birds' migration north
unabated.
Listen there, that one's a male late in spring without a mate.

He's showing off, just in case, a female, even an old one, will have
him.
Little chance now, but he's full-throated, trying not to show his
desperation.

Jen Edwards

Singles Night at a Trailer Park

Shotguns and coon dogs, stubs of welfare checks line trash cans.
Camo pick-up trucks hide Pabst sweat and Marlboro Reds.
I live in the eggshell pink shoe box with a welcome mat.
Last year the mat grew mold on the bathroom floor.
Now, I'm happy its life serves a dual purpose.
The only resident with a porch decoration is classy.
C-section scar like a cut from a scythe kept me from being a strip-
per.
A home birth would have been cheaper.
The cowboy boots outside click square dance rhythms
on warped wood of family-sized picnic tables.
Men howl at the half-moon, thick women tug at the seams
of their tightest dresses. I watch through bug stains
on my kitchen window. I would like to fall in love.
I'd carry a gun, hidden in the ankle of borrowed boots, in case
the evening turned sour. I could ruin a life the way I love clichés
and the warm sound of false promises. Money eases the pain
of departure. The cool green slides between my fingers
like aloe for a burn. It's the end of the world here. A snow globe
people die to get out of. We bang heads against knobby knees
of next door neighbors. We try to knock sense into each other.

Lois Harrod

Why I am Not a Famous Poet

Janine Pommy Vega, Restless Poet, Dies at 68. New York Times, January 3, 2011.

Because Janine Pommy, age sixteen, read Jack Kerouac's *On the Road* and knew immediately that all the characters had an intensity that was missing in her life

> while I, age sixteen, fell asleep trying to read *Death Comes for the Archbishop*.

Because Janine Pommy read a magazine article about the Beats and headed straight for the Cedar Tavern in Greenwich Village, where she met Gregory Corso and Ginsberg and Orlovsky, who became her first lover

> while I shared a tongueless kiss will Bill Carabellos, who wanted to be a Baptist minister.

Because right after her valedictory speech Janine Pommy walked out of Union City High School, New Jersey, and became a waitress in Café Bizarre

while I remained in the lobby of Hubbard High School, Hubbard, Ohio, happy because a few parents were telling me how much they loved my valedictory speech with its abundant alliteration.

Because Janine Pommy wore baggy men's clothes and a stocking cap

while at the little Christian College where my father sent me, I had to dress for dinner. No slacks or jeans, except on Saturday, when there were no classes.

Because Janine Pommy fell in love with the Peruvian painter Fernando Vega and became Janine Pommy Vega (she was still conventional enough to marry the guy and take his name)

  while I fell in love with a history professor who left my virginity intact to become a Catholic priest.

Because Janine Pommy Vega lived the Bohemian life in Paris where she passed the hat for a folk singer and worked as a model at the École de Beaux-Arts

  while I wrote a dissertation on the nesting habits of owls and nightingales as portrayed in a medieval débat poem.

Because Fernando, Janine Pommy Vega's husband, overdosed on heroin on Ibiaz

  while my husband lived on cheap beer in Trenton.

Because Janine Pommy Vega published her first book *Poems to Fernando* with Ferlinghetti at City Lights

  while I published my first book *Every Twinge a Verdict* with Herman Ward at Belle Mead Press.

Because Janine Pommy Vega roamed the world on spiritual quests that took her trekking in the Himalayas and hermiting on the Isla del Sol on Lake Titicaca in Bolivia

  while I stayed at home with two children who thought Titicaca was the funniest word in the English language.

Because while Janine Pommy Vega was writing *Tracking the Serpent* which chronicled her visits to matriarchal power sites in the Amazon, Nepal, France, and Britain

while I was teaching high school English to put my children
through college.

Because Janine Pommy Vega was teaching poets in prisons

and I was teaching poets who only thought they were in prison.

Because she wrote *Mad Dogs or Trieste* and *The Green Piano*

and I. . .

Oh? You never heard of Janine Pommy Vega either? Well . . .

Marco on the Beach

"Dammit," Sara says, Pippin apples spilling out of the broken plastic bag and rolling across the grocery store aisle in a green fan. She bends down, trying to grab them, but Marco sees that she will never find a couple, one lodged under the melon stand, another behind a garbage can. He should kick them out from their hiding places, but he stands and watches the rest roll away. A store employee walks over, smiling the fake smile his boss hands him in the morning along with the green apron he wears.

"It's okay, ma'am," he says, picking up apples. "I'll get them."

Sara turns to Marco, shooting him a terrible look of hate. She's only twenty-five and must not have been ma'amed before.

"Ma'am?" she mouths.

"I'm getting some red wine," Marco says, walking toward the booze aisle.

"Don't get the totally cheap stuff," she says. "It gives me a haircut."

Marco stares at her, noting the dark half moons of smudge under her eyes. She hasn't been sleeping well at night, pulling the blankets over her, tossing them off, the bed an earthquake of quilts. Now she stares blankly at Marco, her expression empty for a second, as if her soul had been abducted by aliens. Then she's transported back. She shrugs, shakes herself, as if trying to find the right word inside her.

"I mean headache. It gives me a headache."

Marco nods, leaves her to the apples. With their remaining food stamps for the month, he can only afford the cheap stuff, so he imagines that Sara isn't going to feel any better later than she does now.

He walks the aisle, seeing over the top into the next. In eighth grade, Marco was five-foot two, compact, a soccer player in white shorts and cleats. But by the time he loped down the echoing high school hall as a freshman, he was nearly six feet, wearing all new clothes and size twelve shoes. On the day of graduation, he was six-foot seven, and even eight years later, he's still not used to the length of his bones, part of him still that tiny guy not picked for basketball during seventh grade phys ed, the kid who could wear the same jeans for two years. When his friends drive him to meetings and political marches, he clambers into cars, hits his head on door jambs and on the tops of car cabins, smashing himself up to fit in, his knees pressed up into his chest in the tiny back seats.

"You unfold like a new moth," Sara said once to him as they got out of the car. He held his arms out to his sides, feeling more albatross than moth-like, able to take flight at any moment and stay aloft forever.

He's even too tall for shopping, having to bend down to look at all the bottles of cheap red wine, the kind that the store sells under stupid names. Stupid names seem to make people laugh, and laughing seems to make people buy stuff. He pulls out a bottle of Chicken Little Winery Cabernet Sauvignon and then slides it back. $2.99. The cheapest. A really big headache. He pulls out Live Wire, a California Valley Merlot at $3.99. Better price often equals upgrade in taste sometimes, enough so that he can count on this tasting only partially of bad vinegar. He puts it back and pulls out a Napa Valley Pinot called Blue Truck, a $5.99 special, with a little card written by Chad, the employee of the month: "Lovely oak undertones with a raspberry and chocolate notes. A great deal!"

There are curlicues and little happy faces on the card, which make Marco want to steal the wine instead of paying for it, just to get back at Chad.

Marco stands straight, holds the Blue Truck in his hand, staring at nothing for a second but the cork ends of wine bottles. He feels angry about the spilled apples and the wine. He feels bad about the haircut, the headache, and the price of everything. He doesn't want to walk back to Sara and help her finish shopping. He might even want to take his stolen bottle of wine and their Mazda and leave the store, the parking lot, maybe even town. His long, lean body itches with desire, but then Sara is next to him. She's tall, too, her shoulder hitting his bicep. She smells like the produce aisle, sharp like pineapple rinds, ripe like tomatoes headed for the dumpster. Her fingertips probably feel like the skins of fallen Pippins.

"It's not the cheapest?" she asks.

"No," Marco says. "Three tiers above migraine."

"Maybe it will just feel like a sinus infection," she says.

"What's this headache bit?" he says, forcing himself not to say *haircut.* "When did that start?"

Sara shrugs, takes the wine bottle, and puts it in their cart. "It doesn't matter. I'm just not going to drink anymore."

"Why?" he asks, but she's already ahead of him, pushing the cart up the aisle toward dairy, a section they shop in now that Sara has given up on being a vegan. The two years of no eggs and cheese made Marco cranky and even thinner, though sometimes he would sneak out and have a steak at Sizzler. Sara would catch him, tell him that his sweat smelled of flesh and synthetic hormones, the kind they shoot into innocent calves the second they are born. She made him drink purifying teas and take baths in Epsom salts, his feet looking like pale, boiled prunes after the long soaks she prescribed.

But one day, Sara just looked at him across the table and said, "I want an omelet."

That was that.

Now, she loads up the cart with butter, cottage cheese, yogurt, and milk. Sometimes when they have some extra cash, she tells him to pick out a rib eye steak. "One that's marbled," she says. "No filets or strips."

Sara has started to crave fat, though she's as lean as Marco. When they lie flat on their backs in their bed, Marco often wonders

68

if from above they look like flooring planks, long stretches of ash or oak or maple.

And lately, Sara seems to be craving more things with strong tastes: peppery arugula with roasted red beets and goat cheese; oily white anchovies from small, glass jars; Italian cheeses at room temperature slathered on black olive sour dough, the cheese so runny there's more need to pour than spread it.

"What about bread?" Marco asks, needing to get out of dairy, the so-white milk cartons and bottles and white dairy tubs of everything suddenly seeming like the segregated, white part of the South.

Sara nods and then begins to study the organic butter. Marco turns and strides down an aisle, turning right and then walking up, landing in front of the grainy, healthy-looking breads, the names of which sport words and phrases like *whole* and *sprouts* and *trans-fat free*.

He puts a hand on a loaf, feeling the soft girth under his palm. He knows he could squeeze hard and like that feeling, remembering the squish of Wonderbread in his hands. One year back in grammar school, he'd gotten his paws on a fresh loaf, probably at some kind of assembly titled "The Work People Do" or "Our Friend Bread" or something lame like that. He can still conjure the bread delivery man in his white uniform and stiff white hat standing on the stage, speaking to them about yeast and freshness. At the end of his fifteen minutes, he must have handed out free products to all the kids, the Wonderbread company banking on the realities of processed white flour addiction. That, and the Wonderbread bags were colorful, big red and blue balloon shapes, the name full of air.

That soft press of flour and eggs under the malleable plastic bag is fresh in his brain, this current loaf almost telling him to go ahead and *do it* like some animated Alice in Wonderbread story: *Squeeze me.*

Marco knows that bread murder is not looked upon kindly by the workers in the store, and probably the guy from the produce aisle would catch him and call the manager, who would dream of calling the cops to report a food murder. The truth is he and Sara should be arrested for a few things, that's for sure. Like using the FedEx number of a huge company to mail things around the country: CDs to Marco's sister Rafaela and brother Fred. Like applying for and getting food stamps when they could be working instead. For embezzling money from Sara's father's janitorial supply company, small, steady amounts that fund their cravings for cheese, their Netflix account, and travel to a funky motel in Pismo Beach in the summer. Seventy-five dollars a night and an all-you-can-eat breakfast buffet.

If there is a scam, he and Sara have surfed it to wave's end. If there is something to take, they have taken it. They don't steal close to home, but everywhere else, it's a matter of course. Walmart is like an oasis from poverty, a barn of goods offered up for the taking, shining, needed objects in heaps and piles. But even a Rite Aid will do, small items slipped into slick pockets. Marco chips away at the consumer culture by consuming for free.

One winter, when Marco was home in the Bay Area visiting during the holidays, his mother Claire pulled him aside and told him, "Look, I don't want a stolen present. If you are going to give me something, make it. Or buy me nothing, okay?"

So instead of stealing picture frames and glittery earrings, he started giving her pencil sketches of the family home or making tomatillo salsa during get-togethers. And rather than stealing, he finds the shiny novels Claire likes when he dumpster dives at the mall, a bookstore now going bankrupt dumping a ton of books every month just because of little tears in the covers.

"Why don't you do something?" his mother asked. "You have a college degree, for god's sake, Marco. We always thought you'd—okay, I hate to say this—we thought you'd *be* something."

A couple of years back, this would have hurt his feelings, and he'd lash out at her. He'd argue, reciting all that he was doing and still is. He and Sara work at the free space they helped create with other local activists, a warm, dry cafeteria-sized place for the homeless to get a cup of coffee, a site for hourly babysitting for low income families. He writes for the local anarchist newspaper and helps deliver it to coffee shops and indie bookstores. He agitates. He goes to open meetings at city hall. He protests the war, military deployments, immigration laws. He reads, and at night, he writes long novels no one but Sara has read.

Marco knows he is something. He's someone, even if he is irritable.

"I'm twenty six," he finally told his mother. "I'm still doing this, so I think this is what I'm going to do forever."

When he spoke the words, they were true. He likes not working at a place, a company, a business, every single day his own to bend like a warm pretzel. Maybe the pretzel wasn't actually warm or even edible, but it was all his.

There was no way to explain this to his librarian mother, and maybe she was as sick of the argument as he was. Now that he thinks about it, Marco hasn't talked to her in months. He hasn't spoken with his father or siblings either, he realizes, a fact that was nonexistent until it was *pow*, here, right now, as he stares at bread.

His stomach growls. He yanks up a loaf up by its plastic neck and walks back toward Sara and the cart, ready to go home and eat.

Sara's favorite scent is patchouli. She sprinkles it in the water at the laundromat before the rinse cycle. Three laundromats have banned them, the next customers using their machines having complained.

"I smelled like a freaking hippie," Marco heard one lady whine. "Like I'd been smoking pot around back of a Quonset hut or something."

Sara switched to lavender after that, but now she's given up on both, their clothes smelling like nothing but clothes. As they sit at the table eating tuna sandwiches, Marco realizes that for the first time in years, he can smell his food and not his shirt.

"Tacoma is so over," she says, wiping her mouth and sitting back. She ate her entire sandwich in about three minutes, and now she seems kind of glazed, everything but her wide eyes wrapped in gauze.

Marco doesn't say anything because his mouth is full. They've lived in Tacoma since they graduated from Evergreen State College and moved out of Olympia, Olympia so over about three years ago. As far as he can see, Highway 101 connects the dots of the three Pacific Rim states. There's Seattle, Portland, San Francisco, and Los Angeles. Anywhere else in between the dots is so over, maybe never even was.

He swallows a gulp of Blue Truck and wishes he were drinking one of the flat but free beers he recovered from behind the Liquor Barn three nights before.

"Where do you want to go?" he asks.

"Sacramento," Sara says.

He blinks, takes another bite of his sandwich. Depending on the season, Sacramento is hot, flat, and ugly or foggy, flat, and ugly. It smells like canals and peat and seems like the end of the world, even though if you face east, it's just the beginning.

"Because of your mom?" Marco asks, putting down his sandwich, his stomach lurching from too much mayonnaise.

Sara nods, shrugs. "She says we can live in her rental. That one on Fourth Street."

Marco graduated with a degree in English, so he's not a total idiot. It's clear that Sara has had preemptive and lengthy phone calls with her mother about this move that already seems to be in the works. Long divorced from Sara's father Hal, Donna teaches anthropology at the university. All Sara's growing up years, she spent summers at digs in Umbria or on cultural missions to Cuba or South Africa. Donna's house presents as a multicultural knickknack exhibit; the living room alone is a mixed metaphor, a tract house room wearing a dashiki and Peruvian wool scarves, everything fluid and colorful but totally square in its tract-ness. And if Marco is honest, Donna looks as though she should be hawking Wonderbread, her hair a vivid, vibrant, dark, lustrous orangey red, the color of a circus clown's nose.

But Donna is the only one of their four parents who asks about Marco's and Sara's projects. She's the only one who understands the system and the dehumanizing forces of societal control, slamming her palm on a flat hard surface when Marco tells her stories, yelling, "The goddamn pigs."

Unlike Claire, Donna throws back shooters of most adult beverages, can hold her liquor but not her tongue. Unlike Claire, Donna doesn't ask Marco what he's going to do with his life, seeming to assume he already has one.

If Marco had to be trapped in a broken elevator with anyone from his or Sara's family, he would pick Donna.

But move to Sacramento?

"Why do you suddenly want to leave Tacoma?" he asks and then takes another bite of his sandwich. Of course, he isn't sure most of the time why he's in Tacoma at all. Sometimes as he looks down Main Street, he thinks the bleak ugliness of the city makes him believe in the possibility of change. Nothing could look as gray and dreary and metallic as this forever.

"I'm pregnant," Sara says and she begins to weep the minute she's said the words.

Marco looks at her, knowing there are eighteen smart things he should do at this moment, but he can't think of the right one. He could lean over and grab her hand. He could get his ass up out of the chair, walk around the table, and pull her into his arms, just like all the douche bags do in movies. She would grab him around the shoulders, bury her head into him, her lips near his neck, the sound of her tears in his ear. He could say something like, "That's wonderful," because it is, kind of, the miracle of life and all that. He feels that miracle, actually, a ripple of adrenaline inside him, the idea that they are going to have a baby.

But he's frozen on his chair, his mouth still full of tuna. He needs to swallow, so he does, but still words don't come. His legs won't move. He's frozen man in a stupid pose.

Now, he thinks. Do it. Do the right thing right now. Tell her you will move to Sacramento and live in Donna's rental. Tell her how happy you are. Tell her that you love her.

But Marco doesn't because only one of the above is true, and maybe not even.

As he watches her, he sees the old people they will be. They will sit at another table the same way, eating the same kind of food, probably. They will have an okay house in a marginal part of some flat, foggy town. Maybe Stockton, maybe Lodi. Their two kids— they will have another after this first unwanted one—will have left the house, moved on to things better because their grandma Donna left them college money. Marco's mother took the kids on vacations after Marco's father died, Marco's kids knowing more about Europe than he ever will.

Marco's hair has fallen out just like his grandfather's, giving him that Friar Tuck look. Sara has grown thinner, paler, and started smoking outside after dinner about ten years into their wedding in South Lake Tahoe. Her lips have that lined, skinny-woman pucker. The only thing in this view that still seems like Sara are her gray eyes, but at this future table, she's always pissed off at Marco, so her gaze at him is dark. After moving to Donna's rental, Marco went back to school for his teaching credential, his entire career spent at the local junior high school teaching kids the five-paragraph essay.

He doesn't think about changing the world with words or creating a new society based on communal goals anymore. He doesn't write his novels, and he doesn't steal, though Walmart still gives him itchy palms.

On the weekend, he watches television and plays pool with his best friend Joe in the basement.

He's still tall of course, but he lugs around a basketball-sized stomach over his belt.

He turned into his father, but not as successful. Or even as nice.

Marco's new life moves with Powerpoint efficiency, ending with shots of the urn on the shitty mantel in he and Sara's shitty house. After a year of wedded bliss, her second husband takes the urn and puts it in the garage next to Marco's old textbooks and propaganda. The urn grows dingy, and, during an earthquake one hot summer afternoon, it tips over, Marco spilling out the garage floor in a plume of gray dust.

Marco's heart pounds against his ribs, his throat dry. His feet feel very large on the floor, as though he were wearing skis. Sara is still weeping, so there's time for him to save things. He can go toward her and make her happy, or he can push his chair back and walk out of the kitchen, the house, the city, the state. He can take Highway 101 down the coast, landing on the dot that most appeals. Maybe Los Angeles. He can apply to graduate school and write a screenplay about his ragged, anarchical Tacoma life. He can become famous and write more scripts and live in Malibu. He can give into the lure of society and roll around in it like it was bacon fat. Marco imagines the girlfriends he will have, all blonde and not as tall as Sara. He will get a vasectomy as soon as he makes his first million. He will start producing movies, too, and people will call him about how to make the fake look real. Marco knows how to do this, so he'll become the go-to guy for advice.

Every Oscar night, his films will win awards, and the stumbling nervous famous people on the stage will thank him. Meanwhile, he'll drink a beer on the beach in a comfy lounge chair and watch rain on the winter sea. And that's how he will die, Marco, on the beach, his maid finding him in the morning, the beer gone, a smile on his face.

As he listens to Sara cry, the man in his head bats the air with his hands, searching for the gray answer, the one in the middle, the answer that Goldilocks would pick, something just right. Neither teacher nor screenwriter, not poor or rich, not famous or just nothing. Doing something but not everything. Changing the world but only one day at a time.

Who is that gray, middle Marco? Where is the Marco who doesn't squish the Wonderbread but doesn't eat it either? Where is the man who would walk into a business, hang up his jacket, and get to work?

Sara lifts her head, the question in her eyes. She waits for him to do something. So does Marco, his breath caught in his body, the answer one exhale away.

John G. Rodwan, Jr.

One Hundred and Ten Boxes

The date did not do it. We did not leave New York when we did because of what happened there precisely seven years earlier. September 11, 2008, was a Thursday, the day of the week that alternate side of the street parking opened space on what for several years had been our side of the street. Street-cleaning-related rules briefly created an opening for a large truck to stop near a building in need of emptying. For people moving, such practical matters take precedence over symbolism.

While logistical considerations guided our relocation schedule-making, the date did intrude on our thoughts. After our belongings had been hauled away, my wife Nancy and I went and sat at John F. Kennedy airport waiting to board our flight to the other side of the country. The required display to uniformed agents of plastic bags containing circumscribed quantities of toiletries, the shuffle through metal detectors on shoeless feet, and the other rituals of security implemented early in the twenty-first century—these alone would have provided plenty of reminders of what day it was. After one of our earlier, exploratory trips to Portland, we discovered that the guardians of air transportation in New York had permitted us to carry a knife onto the plane. Swiss Army knives had been a regular part of our travel gear back when flyers did not have to consider the condition of their socks, whether they had more than three ounces of shampoo, or if they had eminently useful combinations of bottle and can opener, food slicer and repair kit in their carry-on luggage. We had not intended to bring the versatile tool with us; it had simply been left in a bag routinely and forgotten until we discovered it while unpacking in the hotel. Nancy had bought this particular knife in Switzerland when we lived there. Rather than test whether Oregon's luggage x-rayers were more diligent than their New York counterparts and risk losing the souvenir, we mailed it back East.

We changed coasts during presidential campaign season. The televisions hanging from ceilings throughout the airport terminal broadcast the joint hand-shaking and picture-taking event candidates Barack Obama and John McCain staged where the Twin Towers had stood for almost thirty years. The political rivals walked together in the afternoon sun at what for many years had been a massive concrete lined hole.

We had been past the same void ourselves, though we never deliberately went to look at the devastation. Our first close-up glimpse of the mass-murder site had been inadvertent. We were not making any sort of pilgrimage when we exited a subways station and found ourselves looking at homemade signs posted on every available upright surface near that hole. They showed pictures of the missing whom others still had hope, then, of finding alive. We had an out-of-town visitor who wanted to see something else in that part of Lower Manhattan, and, in another case of the practical trumping the symbolic, we had simply taken the most direct route to get there. Another time, we had not asked the livery cab driver to take us through that part of town on the way from Brooklyn to the airport in Newark, New Jersey, but that was the route he chose, making sure we would think about the still-recent catastrophe on our first post-September 11th flight. We would have thought about it anyway, I'm sure.

We did not avoid the World Trade Center zone out any sort of indifference or callousness. Rather, it had not been an area we frequented when the complex existed. We knew people who worked there. During our time living in the city, I had been inside the building only twice, I think, and even then I had not gone up inside either tower. Once I simply went underneath to reach a train. The World Trade Center formed the only part of the city's storied skyline that we could see from our first apartment in Brooklyn, and that was Nancy's vantage point when I telephoned to tell her what had happened to it that fall morning. Before then, if I happened to look up from my book and gaze out the window, I would notice it when trains crossed the East River on the Manhattan Bridge, but

I never though much about the place until it was gone. There had been a distance, both literally and figuratively, between me and it. The idea of going to see that hole seemed inappropriate, unearned, like visiting the grave of a stranger, or, more accurately, thousands of strangers.

We lived in New York longer after than before the obliteration of the structure and many of its occupants. Much like we did with our first walk past what became known as Ground Zero, we ended up in the city but not because of any particular desire to be there. When in Switzerland, Nancy and I both worked on the same publishing project. Near its completion this involved working in New York. Once we were finished, we found other work and stayed. We did not arrive there as part of a conscious plan and never envisioned it as a permanent home. Just as we had in Geneva, we resided in New York with the knowledge that eventually we would go somewhere else.

The city offered as many reasons to stay as to go, as many reasons to go as to stay. Close-standing subway riders; unknown-but-still-despised neighbors who mercilessly expose other tenants to their noise; side-walk-blocking, stop-and-go baby stroller pushers; long-leash dog walkers; out-of-step tourists; assertively unaware residents; and geniuses who behave as if keeping the rat population thriving on samplings of the world's cuisines were an urban pastime if not a civic duty—these irritants did not motivate us to leave. Unforgettable concerts in small rooms in TriBeCa, Greenwich Village and the Lower East Side and in stately halls uptown; readings by admired authors; plays and operas at Lincoln Center and the Brooklyn Academy of Music; championship boxing at Madison Square Garden; unsurpassable meals at places within walking distance from our apartment, at Michelin Guide-endorsed restaurants engineered by Thomas Keller, and at tradition-bound steak houses; and the regular exposure to varieties of real geniuses —these did not persuade us to stay.

New York may offer the world, but it also makes residents want to tune it out. A large number of people in a small amount of space—the very thing that makes the vitality of the city's cultural life possible—encourages willful obliviousness as a way of coping with others' unbearable nearness. Dealing with the inevitable intrusiveness of others this way escalates inconsideration: when almost everyone behaves as if no one else matters, then only the misguided or the saintly willingly act like the sucker who gives a damn. This discourages basic decency (which survives only as an eccentricity noteworthy mainly for its rareness) and promotes humans' worst impulses, including an aggressive, intentional disregard for others. New Yorkers routinely behave as if no one else walks with them on the crowded sidewalk and no one lives on the other side of the wall. Even as it encourages a ceaselessly reinvigorated and reinvigorating cultural bonanza, New York has a coarsening and dulling effect over time.

People need to move away from "the same worn-out soil" in order thrive, Nathaniel Hawthorne asserts in the passage in *The Custom House* from which Jhumpa Lahiri takes the title of *Unaccustomed Earth*, one of the last books we obtained before imposing a pre-move moratorium. We had responded to the impetus for unsettlement before. One summer before we were married, Nancy and I took two months and drove around the country, traveling almost nine thousand miles through twenty-two states. On a freeway in Arizona we glimpsed the aftermath of a fiery accident involving eighteen-wheelers, including a residential mover's truck, which almost certainly instilled a subsequent wariness over subjecting everything we owned to such a possible end. On our first wedding anniversary, we flew to Switzerland, where a six-month stint at the United Nations agency grew to last for more than a year. While there, we traveled as frequently as possible, moving through a dozen countries. We used weekends and what by American standards was a luxurious amount of vacation time to see as much as we could. After more than decade in New York, we decided we were ready to see—to be—somewhere else. I remember hearing that Americans, a nation of wanderers, move more often than people in other countries, and it felt time that we do our part to uphold the transitory tradition.

Over the course of a few weeks, piles of cardboard boxes grew around out apartment. We numbered each box with a black Sharpie and kept an inventory so we would be able to unpack efficiently. If we wanted to know where we had stowed the wall clock, bathroom garbage can, hair dryer, refrigerator magnets, battery-powered lantern, bike lock and chain, blank-page books and power strips, we would be ready (and when the box that actually did have such contents—number forty-one—and the others arrived, we were). When we taped shut the last carton, the total had reached 110.

The 110 boxes did not hold everything. A couple weeks before our September 11th departure (but after the one with the knife), we took a path-clearing trip to Portland. We rented a car and went shopping. Having the new place stocked with cooking oil and canned goods, batteries and cleaning supplies, a mop and a broom, a new vacuum cleaner and toilet paper would mean not having to go get all those elemental things while also trying to unpack and set up. It would be nice, we knew, to arrive and already have some meat in the freezer and cold beer in the refrigerator. We also got mundane dealings with banks and insurance companies out of the way. We made sure we had food and litter for the cats. Before leaving Brooklyn, we selected several things we did not want to entrust to the movers. These were not items of exceptional monetary value. We took our dessert-island favorites: music, movies and books. Even if everything else we owned got lost or destroyed, we would still have sustaining listening, watching and reading. All of that, along with a coffee pot, a laptop computer and the clothes we also left on that preliminary expedition, would have filled a couple more boxes if they had not gone in suitcases. We sent things we wanted to receive sooner (another computer, a bicycle) separately by a faster method after we were told that our 110 boxes (as well as the furniture) could take more than a week to get to Oregon.

Another moving company estimate also affected what was ultimately delivered or, more accurately, what was not. Nancy and I had never thought of ourselves as thing-people. Our aesthetic favored the utilitarian over the decorative; we did not clutter our places with knickknacks, framed snapshots or other unnecessary dust-catchers. Besides, while Brooklyn's apartments may boast more square footage per dollar than Manhattan's, many of them still do not include much storage space. We had friends who did not have even a single closet. Such living quarters discourage hording. Or so I thought. As devoted readers, we had walls lined with bookcases. We did have closets, including one large enough for a file cabinet filled with old bank statements, bills and canceled checks. Our shredder broke before we could destroy all our unneeded documents filled with personal information.

We had another, more reliable method of dispensing of other, less private inessentials: the stoop sales that were part of culture in the neighborhood where we lived. On clear days in spring, summer and fall, residents would put books and baby clothes, furniture and toys, pans and pots, shoes and picture frames out on the steps and sidewalks in front of their brownstones and sell them. Frequently, as morning turned to afternoon and the quantity and appeal of used items diminished, sellers would become givers. They would leave what they did not want to take back inside their homes for passersby to haul into theirs. When we decided to go, we had to purge.

Relocating concentrates the mind on how people never stop paying for what they own. The simple transaction related to purchasing an item is the beginning of spending, not the end. After that, we pay to shelter or store what we bought. A key consideration in picking a place to live is whether it has room not only for people but also for their stuff. All those bookcases demand a room of their own. Insurance adds still more costs. When it comes time to take what has been acquired from one place to another, purported owners confront decisions about how much they are willing to continuing paying for their things. Even after selling what we deemed unworthy of taking across the country, and pitching what we should never have held onto in the first place, movers quoted prices that made us reconsider yet again what we thought we really wanted or needed. All those unused glasses might once have seemed worth keeping for large parties we never threw but now they revealed themselves to be unnecessary extravagances. Certain pieces of furniture and electrical appliances fit that classification too. Closets, it turns out, too easily hold clothes that don't fit or are never worn. So we held a second, even larger stoop sale.

While we had sold or given away books before, it never had been easy to part with them—until we learned what it would cost to keep them. Movers set their fees by weight, and book collections are heavy. Instantly those anthologies held onto since college became undeserving of the ongoing rent paid to keep housing them. Lahiri's title story involves a father who declines to share the large house in the Pacific Northwest where his daughter and husband moved from Park Slope, Brooklyn. He prefers to remain in his small condominium because he likes the freedom from "all the things he'd recently gotten rid of, all the books and papers and clothes and objects one felt compelled to possess, to save." We did not entirely free ourselves of years of accumulated things, but we did shed a good amount. In preparing for that second sale, we aggressively sought more and more to jettison. When we first started the reduction process, I worried that we might rashly dispose of thing we would later wish we still had. I got over that. Breaking the compulsion to possess felt liberating. No one whose belongings exceed what fits in 110 boxes can claim to have slipped the shackles of materialism, but I know that the figure would have been much more absurdly large had we not gotten a sense of the freedom enjoyed by Lahiri's character.

Our earlier episodes of rootlessness did not present the same challenges that our escape from New York posed. Alternating between campgrounds and cheap motels during an aimless cross-country ramble is easy when you are between semesters in graduate school or have job you would happily quit. Abandoning a menial editing job for one paying a salary four times larger (and tax free) in the middle of Europe is easy too. Then, we did not own anywhere near enough to fill one hundred and ten boxes. We fit all we wanted into a few suitcases. We lived in furnished apartments. Abruptly changing course in middle age, especially with no new source of income, takes a greater effort of will.

For all the practical considerations surrounding the move

—when to go, what to take —a major concern for me had been the wisdom of going at all. I knew that I wanted something else, a new set of experiences, another way of living, an unfamiliar landscape —unaccustomed earth!—but I also wrestled with an unexpected reluctance. The state of the economy worried voters more than, say, the war in Iraq or any other single issue at the time of the election, according to polls cited in news reports. Was this the time to make a change? Were we being imprudent? When I hesitated to commit to the plan—and I did hesitate—was I simply succumbing to fear?

Paradoxically, perhaps, recognizing that I felt scared made deciding what to do much easier. To stay put would mean living with the shame of submitting to a familiar but unsatisfying routine because of an ignoble unwillingness to hazard anything to break out of it. So what if, as I feared, the next place proved only different and not obviously better? Different was the point, and different was good enough. Perhaps flinging ourselves across country did not make sense financially—another possible reason for caution. Or inaction. Did I really want that to determine how I lived? We went somewhere new this time because we chose to rather than out of economic necessity or because an unforeseen opportunity arose. The move could be tightly choreographed, but the reason for making it did not need to be straightforwardly sensible. Once I realized that the best reason to replant ourselves was because we wanted to and could, we did.

Although the events of September 11, 2001, did not drive us out of New York, they did affect how we lived there for seven years afterwards. Catastrophes cause demands for action. The appearance of a concerted response must satisfy some human need even if it does not actually solve the catalyzing problems. When covering the 1968 Republican convention in Miami, Norman Mailer noticed "echoes" of the then-recent assassination of Robert Kennedy in showy measures that provided no actual protection for candidates. When Nelson Rockefeller's airplane arrived, helicopters circled the airport as heavily armed police patroled on the ground. Yet Mailer never needed to show any identification to guards. He realized that a would-be killer pretending to be a journalist could have easily carried a gun within a few feet of New York's governor. Such an assassin never would have gotten away, Mailer conceded, but he still could have hit his target, since the forces arrayed offer "no real security, just powers of retaliation." Forty years later, some things had changed, but much had not. After September 11th, going anywhere without photo ID became much harder, but weaknesses in pretenses of security persisted. The echoes of September 11th involved police periodically standing at tables next to subway turnstiles and occasionally stopping passengers to look in their bags. Machine-gun-equipped troops were widely deployed, and helicopters endlessly circled above, and not only at airports or when politicians moved through town. Yet if murderers plan on not escaping with their lives, then such armed pageants have no deterrent effect. Retaliatory powers do not matter to terrorists eager to obliterate themselves along with their victims. If a bomber willing to kill himself and numerous strangers failed to board the subway but were instead to self-detonate at a checkpoint, decimating multiple police officers as well as commuters, then his fellow fanatics would probably consider the act a success. Even if I did not worriedly look at the gap in the skyline while traveling into or out of Manhattan, I knew while riding in crowded trains that if terrorists wanted to explode themselves and others during rush hour, they could. I never developed the New Yorker's capacity to pretend unpleasant realities did not exist or that other people's action did not affect me. The random search charade provides nothing more than the illusion of greater safety. Security measures unlikely to do any more than give a modicum of comfort to those who feel that the authorities must "do something" became a part of every New Yorker's routine.

As we adapted to the new age, Nancy and I also started documenting our lives more carefully, considering them more closely and reflecting on them more intently. George Orwell, whose nonfiction I carried by hand to our new home out West, was a list-maker. He said he had "the sort of mind that takes pleasure in dates, lists, catalogues, concrete details, descriptions of processes, junk-shop windows, and back numbers" of old magazines. As our precise accounting of all we owned attests, Nancy and I both have that kind of mind too. Like Orwell, we started writing down every book we read each year. Trying to reassemble 2001's reading proved challenging. After several weeks or months go by, recalling precisely when a book was read becomes difficult. In subsequent years we updated our individual bibliographies whenever we had a new book to add, noting the month when we finished each one. One of Orwell's biographers called the compilation of lists "a strange kind of addiction," and it can indeed be habit-forming. Eventually, we started keeping other lists: compact discs purchased, movies seen (in theaters on one list, at home on another), restaurants dined in and shows seen. While others attended the same events, dined where we enjoyed meals, heard the same people talk, read the same books, heard the same recordings and watched the same movies (somewhere), our particular arrangement of experiences comprises our private histories. Lists like ours assist the memory, permitting their makers to recall experiences they otherwise might have forgotten. They also provide ways to assess states of existence by documenting how the list-keepers spent their time.

In Europe I would have called my passport my most valued possession because of where it made it possible for me to go. Later the volume Nancy and I refer to simply as The Book subsequently got that designation for preserving where we have been and what we have done amid our serial deracinations. The blue-spined journal with sewn-in ribbon bookmark filled with lists did not get packed in any of the one hundred and ten boxes. It came with us on a plane to a fresh patch of unaccustomed earth.

Pinckney Benedict

Damselfly

"And the shapes of the locusts were like unto horses prepared unto battle; and on their heads were as it were crowns like gold, and their faces were as the faces of men. And they had hair as the hair of women, and their teeth were as the teeth of lions. And they had breastplates, as it were breastplates of iron; and the sound of their wings was as the sound of chariots of many horses running to battle."

Revelation 9:7-9

At just past four in the morning, with the false dawn brightening the eastern sky, Nimrod Nickel once again found himself wide awake. He sat in the place where he'd watched the sun rise every morning for a week or more: perched on a hard wooden chair turned backward, arms crossed on the chair's rigid back, staring out of his open kitchen window, praying for a breeze. Anything—a sigh, a whisper, a kiss. Anything but this apparently endless doldrums. The suffocating summer's heat and the constant droning of the seventeen-year locusts had bored their way deep into his brain, and he felt like at any minute he might go mad. At any moment, he might explode into flames. He might scream. He might hurl the kitchen chair through the screen door that opened onto the back porch. He might even do a worse thing. *Give me something*, he thought. His voice no more than a whisper, he said, "Anything."

Out in his back yard, not far from the old smokehouse, some thing moved. It was slight and pale and it walked upright. Nimrod squinted. Sweat dripped from his furrowed brow into his eyes, and he wiped at it. A child? A girl? The salt of his sweat stung him, and his vision momentarily dimmed and swam. The pale figure—pale wasn't the right word for it, exactly; it seemed luminous, it seemed almost to *glow*—crossed the bottom of his yard with its flitting, light-footed gait and, quick as a wink, brushed open the door of the smokehouse and slipped inside.

For a moment, Nimrod imagined that the glow he had seen—a blue luminescence as pure as light refracted from the faces of a diamond, as calm as the rays of the late-afternoon sun glancing off the surface of a cool, deep lake—outlined the heavy wooden door of the ramshackle smokehouse. How bright must that radiance be, to shine through the gap around the door that way? Inside the smokehouse, which hadn't seen any proper use since his grandfather's time, it must be blinding, he imagined. Nimrod closed his smarting eyes and held them closed, and when he opened them again, his vision had cleared. There was no figure, no girl, no glow.

Pharaoh pharaoh pharaoh, cried the locusts in their unnumbered millions. *Pharoah pharaoh pharaoh:* the locusts' two-syllable mating chorus, endlessly repeated from every tree on Nimrod Nickel's place, from every tree in the green little valley that lay beneath the looming shadow of Nickel's Ridge, and from every tree and shrub and bush on the ridge. It was as though the trees themselves were crying out.

The only trees that had been spared the locust infestation were the ones covered in caterpillar cocoons. These trees stood shrouded, silent and ghostly in their white silk garments, amidst the others. Apparently the caterpillars and the locusts had an understanding between them. But the other trees: they were cloaked in the whirring, creeping, buzzing carpet of locusts. *Pharaoh pharaoh pharaoh.* Nimrod Nickel's mother had told him when he was a little boy, when the unrelenting cry of the seventeen-year locusts had frightened him, that they made that sound to remind the world of the fate that had befallen the magnificent Pharaoh of Egypt when he hardened his heart against YWHW, the Lord God of Hosts. The eighth plague, followed by darkness, followed by the Destroyer.

The crushing heat had continued unbroken for better than a month now, not a breath of wind since the day in early summer when the locusts had begun boiling up out of the ground (repulsive, to watch them pull themselves free of the earth, like dead men clawing their way out of their graves; and yet he hadn't been able to look away, fascinated for hours as his land bloomed with this weird, alien crop), and the humidity made him feel weak and woozy and sick to his stomach. He knew he needed to drink water to stay healthy, he had learned that much as a boy and had relearned it during his time in the desert, but still he couldn't bear it. On his tongue, the metallic tang of the tap water—drawn by electric pump from an ancient limestone aquifer four hundred feet below the surface—made him think of blood. He felt his gorge rise, just imagining it. He had grown up in that house, drinking that water, and it had never bothered him before this summer, but now—now it didn't bear thinking about. Like the locusts bursting from every inch of his property. Unbearable.

Needless to say, he wasn't eating well (*You're going to waste away,* his plump, pretty wife, younger than he was by several years, said to him at every meal—*Don't you care for my cooking anymore?*) and he'd begun losing weight, his jeans hanging loose from the sharp angles of his hipbones, his workshirt when he put one on in the morning draping over him like some kind of a caftan. He'd had to punch two extra holes, first one and then another just a week later, in the wide leather belt that he wore, the one with the heavy brass bull's head buckle. He hadn't slept through the night in weeks. He was beginning to see things, movement in the corners of his vision, cobwebs where there weren't any cobwebs, moving shadows when there was no light to throw a shadow and nothing moving to cast it. And now—*had she been naked?*—a girl. A girl had drifted across his yard and gone into the smokehouse.

He'd had visions like these before, seen things that weren't there. In the desert. There too, the heat had seemed likely to drive him mad. The endless patrols. The Dexedrine to get himself up for combat, the Restoril to get to sleep again, *go, no-go,* in an endless, hallucinatory, ever-tightening spiral. He knew he had killed people on some of those patrols, because he had seen the pictures of their sprawled, awkward bodies on the bright screens of his squadmates' cell phones. They had clapped him on the back, his fellow soldiers, and declared their admiration for his fearlessness. *Nimrod*, they had said to him, *you, sir, are a warrior.* All of his people, all of the Nickel men, had been warriors, from the very first one of them, who had fought the Shawnee in this very place. Still, he was damned if he could recall any of it with clarity. The visions, the voices, the glowing girl at the end of his yard—those were clearer than the things that had really happened to him.

He knew that if he went out to the smokehouse, if he threw the door open, the little eight-by-eight cell, with its impossibly thick walls, iron-hard oak log piled on oak log and cemented together with viscous, greasy bitumen—he knew the room would be empty. Some trash and leaf litter in the corners, a few spiders creeping along their silken webs high up among the rafters. Those, and the ghostly pong of curing meat, residue of long-gone salty slabs of bacon and monstrous sides of beef and the muscular loins of whitetail deer, sweating blood, and the rounded forms of ornate pheasants, their feathers gleaming slickly, ripening as they hung by their necks, waiting for their glossy bodies to drop away. "That's when you know the meat is ripe." He heard his grandfather's voice, as though the old man were speaking into his ear. "When the body falls away from the neck." Nimrod cupped a hand over his mouth, queasy again.

All of these things he remembered from his boyhood, his grandfather sweeping open the door and gesturing young Nimrod (*how old had he been? Eight? The age of his own son?*) through, showing him the richness of the interior. "So long as this smokehouse is full, you'll never know want," Nimrod's grandfather had said. His face, the old man's face, had been seamed and pocked, the flesh loose on the bones beneath (as though it might fall away, as though it might finally be *ripe*), and even his grin, full of pride at the sight of all that high meat stored up against an uncertain future, had seemed frightening to young Nimrod: you grew old and you stored up aging meat in a small wooden house in the shadow of Nickel's Ridge, and you yourself were aging meat hidden in that selfsame shadow, and that was what the future held for you. That was what the boy Nimrod had taken away from that little expedition. That, and a taste for store-bought victuals.

As a man, he had never once put meat in the smokehouse. The smokehouse had stood empty through the years that he had owned the place at the foot of Nickel's Ridge. And had he known want? From time to time he had, his family had, but he had always staved it off in one way or another. Mostly by working for other men on their land, because Nimrod Nickel was strong and handy, and it was only with his own land that he seemed to have no luck. For a few years, by joining the service and shooting people in a far-off place, which hadn't paid as well as you might think it would, but which was a trade the men in his family had always followed and in which they had always found success. Thus he had staved off want and, having put it at bay, had returned to his own house, the original house of the Nickel family. That house was a rambling collection of rooms tacked on, at various times and in various styles, to the stalwart log cabin, not so much bigger than the smokehouse, and not so different in its construction, that the first of the Nickel men (another Nimrod, who had spelled his last name with two Ls, *Nickell*) had, in the mid-eighteenth century, erected in this place among the Shawnees, as a trading post and, more often, a fortress.

Nimrod had been mulling over an offer as he sat on the hard kitchen chair and listened to the incessant thrumming of the locusts and prayed for a breeze (was it too much too ask? Just a slight movement of the air, one of the blessed drafts that so often flowed like water from the shoulder of the ridge and down into their little valley) and looked out the window at the log-walled smokehouse that his grandfather, who had also been named Nimrod (*Nimrod was a great hunter before the LORD!*): the offer he was considering, and which had come to him as a complete surprise, was a rich one: an offer for the ridge itself and for the precious seam of soft black coal that lay hidden beneath it.

The Monongahela Consolidated Coal Company would purchase the ridge, if Nimrod agreed, and they would dynamite its top, throw the vast mass of it down into the valley, they would bury this valley with its rambling old house that had belonged to one Nickel and then another and another, generation after generation, great hunters before the LORD, hunters of men, and the land around the house itself, as well as the thick-walled smokehouse (was it empty? Had a girl—a naked girl—dashed in there a moment ago, as light on her feet as a deer or fox? So light that she seemed almost to float over the ground?), and the ancient twisted old oak trees with their burden of chittering, remorseless locusts. They would help the Nickel family to move—where? elsewhere— and they would decapitate the ridge and they would scoop out its valuable heart, they would fill the valley with rubble, and then they would be on their way again, on to the next place. And what of the Nickels? What would become of them?

Yes, there had been want. After this one last sale, though, there would never be want again.

Pharaoh pharaoh pharaoh!

Nimrod's wife didn't seem to have any trouble sleeping. Their son, who was genial and nervous and bucktoothed and bespectacled and skinny as a whippet, constantly grinning at nothing in particular—he didn't seem to have any trouble sleeping either. They were both asleep right at that moment: Nimrod's wife lying on her back amidst a warm tangle of sheets, slightly damp with sweat, in their bedroom next to the kitchen; and the boy atop a thin mattress on the floor of the sleeping porch at the far end of the house.

Even the dogs slumbered, flattened against the floor like hairy rugs. The heat had rendered them unconscious. In that household, only Nimrod Nickel had difficulty staying asleep. He thought for the millionth time of the vial of Ambien that stood on the porcelain of the bathroom sink, untouched since his wife had procured it for him, when he had complained to her about his sleeplessness. He thought of it, and of the Restoril and the Dexedrine, of *go* and *no-go*, of the photographs of the twilight killings that he couldn't even recall; and of the things that fluttered nastily in the periphery of his vision: the terrifying six-winged angels with their burning faces, the hump-backed thick-hided beasts that cavorted and battled and rutted just out of his sight. He wouldn't go that route again.

Maybe it was an escaped prisoner in the smokehouse. They got away, every now and again, from the federal women's prison (the *camp*, they called it, the administrators there—how precious!) ten or so miles away, in an otherwise uninhabited valley to the east. They were mostly city girls inside there, almost all convicted on drug charges, and when they broke out (broke out? When they walked away from the place, because there weren't walls or even fences, really, not of the sort an actual prison would have), they usually followed the highway or the railroad tracks until they got picked up by the state troopers a few hours later. By then they were hungry and tired and ready to go back to the *camp*.

Sometimes the more ambitious among the escapees tried to follow the river or, setting out cross-country, got lost in the deep woods, and when they were finally found, sometimes after a few days, they were footsore and covered in poison oak, hypothermic and half-starved, dehydrated and babbling about the beings that they had seen among the lonely, abandoned hills, yammering on and on about the things the stealthy hill-creatures had said to them, the liberties they had taken.

A few of those ambitious ones, he recalled, hadn't been found at all, and Nimrod figured their bones were scattered on the floor of the forest, their skulls home to rodents and snakes and beetles. So maybe this was one of those pitiful ones, huddling inside his smokehouse, hoping—like a little kid—that someone was going to come and find her and take her back to a place where there was electricity and air conditioning and hot nourishing food and television, and where the sound of the locusts didn't surround you and drill into your head and drive you mad.

He stood up from the chair, considering for a moment whether or not he ought to take the little double-barreled coach gun out there with him. There were two possibilities, he figured: either the smokehouse was empty, or there was some girl—if there was anybody at all, it was someone quite small, and he was a large man, in his physical prime—from Detroit or Fort Lauderdale or some other urban shithole, and she would probably thank him for discovering her and ask to borrow his phone to call the feds to come and get her. He flexed his muscular arms and decided he wouldn't need the gun.

As he threw open the screen door, one of the dogs stirred in its sleep. He waited a moment, to see if it wanted to come with him on his errand, but it subsided, whimpering slightly, back into its dreams. The door slapped shut behind him, and Nimrod stepped out into his yard.

Into cacophony. Inside his house, he'd at least had the sense of human belongings around him, of a human arrangement of objects and spaces, of a place that had been planned by and that made sense to the human brain. Out here, though—out here he understood that he had stepped into the insect world, and his mind reeled. As he made his way toward the smokehouse, the discarded husks of locusts crunched under his feet, and their shrilling song—*Pharaoh pharaoh pharaoh!*—filled his ears, ten times, a hundred times louder than it had been when he sat within his own walls, within the ancestral fortress of the Nickel clan.

The locusts hopped and burrowed and ate and winged their noisy way from tree to tree. Blindly, they batted against his hands and his face, and he struck out at them, even as he understood that there were too many for him ever to rid himself of them. The could not be driven off, so they must be borne. He remembered a teaching saying, in some long-ago junior high science class, that, if you were to put all the people on the planet into one great big garbage bag, and all the insects on the planet into another, the bag containing the insects would weigh several hundred times more than the bag containing the humans. Until this moment, he had always found that statistic difficult to believe.

Even worse than the screaming locusts, though, were the trees—silent, ghostly—that had been shrouded by the tent caterpillars. At least the locusts were *life*. The caterpillars were death, mantling the trees they had chosen in thick webs and then consuming them. Nimrod listened closely and heard, under the shrilling of the locusts, a ticking, clattering sound that came from within the caterpillars' canopy, and he knew that it was the sound of their droppings raining down within the veils of their cocoons. The hidden caterpillars were converting his trees to shit. He peered at the nearest of the tented trees and thought that he could make out, under the white blanket, the creeping shapes of the caterpillars as they went this way and that on the doomed trees branches. It was difficult to tell if it was a million caterpillars in there, or just one vast being made of a million undifferentiated creeping parts.

He had meant to burn out the caterpillars at the beginning of the infestation, had even devised a clever propane wand, a torch with a hissing eight-foot flame, that would have served the purpose handsomely. He had meant to save his trees. But then the locusts had come, and the whole place had been overrun, and there hadn't been a point to it anymore, it had seemed to him. Now, of course, it was too late: he'd have to burn the whole place, set fire to the whole ridge, the whole forest, to get rid of the caterpillars.

He laughed a little. *What will you do,* he thought, *when Monongahela Consolidated buries you? What will you do then, you killers, you ravagers, you obscenities?*

And he found himself at the door of the smokehouse. The wood of the door, the logs of the walls, were thick with locust casings. Nimrod examined one of them that clung to the door at the height of his eyes. It looked, he found, precisely like the living locust that had abandoned it. It was perfect in all of its parts: its nimble legs, it delicate thorax, its bulging eyes; but it was empty and dead. He took it between his thumb and forefinger and tried to pull it away from the door, but it clung fast. Only when he twisted it so that its legs snapped did it come free. In his large palm, it was tiny. It weighed nothing. It gleamed like bronze. He tossed it onto the ground, and when it fell he could not tell it from the ten thousand similar shells that lay there.

He had stood outside doors like this one before. In combat. He had blown doors like this off their hinges and tossed grenades into the rooms inside. He had entered the rooms, M4 chattering in his hands, hot brass shell-casings clattering and spanging off the walls, falling in bright cascades to the floor. He did not recall it, but he knew that he had done it. He was Nimrod Nickel, and the Nickel men were warriors.

Feeling more than a bit silly as he did so, he knocked on the door of the smokehouse. *Shave and a haircut, two bits.* "Is anyone there?" he called. His voice sounded weak and thin to him, nearly drowned out by the shrieking of the locusts. *There are so many of them*, he thought, *and, truly, so few of us. What is to be done?* He thought briefly of the makeshift flamethrower in his garage and knew that his instinct about its futility had been correct. The infestation was here. It was in the land, it lay deep in the earth. It had gestated there for years, blind and squirming. It had been there before him and his kind, and it would be there long after them. It could not be overcome by the artifices of man, no matter how clever. And soon, it would be the problem of Mon Consolidated. They could crack open the vault of the earth if they liked and come to grips with what lay hidden there. "Ready or not, I'm coming in," he called.

No more stalling. He swung wide the smokehouse door, knowing full well that the little outbuilding was empty.

And saw her.

Slender as a young birch. Long-limbed, her posture holding the promise of a superhuman litheness. Narrow, supple waist, surprisingly full breasts. Wide eyes, impossibly wide, and lidless. Nude as the day she was born, and her skin shone like the surface of a pearl. He felt himself drawn to her, more strongly than he had ever been drawn to a woman before, and he felt at the same time the strangeness of that attraction. He was disgusted by it and helpless in the face of it. She smiled at him, and there were things—glistening, mandibular things—revealed by her smile that no human mouth should ever contain. He wanted to flee, but because he had never beheld something so awful and so beautiful before, he stayed rooted to his spot before the open door. She seemed to sense that her smile was disconcerting to him, and her expression became somber, the wriggling mouth-parts hidden behind moist lips.

She was a nymph. That had to be it. And it was *nymph*, wasn't it, that they called the final form of the locust, the one that came up out of the ground? There were other forms too, conjured through a multitude of moltings: larva, pupa, imago—it seemed preposterous to him, somehow, that something as simple as a locust, something not even as big as his thumb, should have so many different forms in the course of its life, and that the great bulk of that life should be lived out in utter darkness and silence, buried in the ground beneath the Nickel place; and that the rest of it should be carried out in his trees, shrieking and shrilling in the great universal competition to find a mate.

Many insects, he recalled from that selfsame science class, from some antique film strip replete with grainy images of burrowing beetles and horned, carapaced things that burrowed in the dirt and ate the flesh of the dead—many insects, perhaps most, had forms that were called *nymph*.

He could almost hear the stentorian voice of the film strip narrator as the images flowed past, a phantasmagoria of a myriad fluttering, buzzing, translucent, venous wings; jewel-like eyes with a thousand depthless facets; spiked feelers and feathery antennae; obscene proboscises furling and unfurling; intricate, wicked appendages; and gleaming, chitinous exoskeletons:

"The nymphs of aquatic insects, as in the orders Odonata–" A cricket click to indicate that the teacher should advance the filmstrip, and now on the screen there stands the image of a dozen multihued dragonflies hovering over a patch of cattails at the edge of an algae-covered pond.

"—Ephemeroptera—" The cricket click again, and a clutch of mayflies whirls through the air, alive for only perhaps a score of hours and then gone forever.

"—and Plecoptera." *Click*, and a swarm of primitive-looking stoneflies clusters thirstily just above the sparkling rapids of a clear, swift-flowing stream.

"The nymphs are also sometimes called *naiads*," continues the narrator, "which is an ancient Hellenic name for the race of mythological water sylphs which would, through the use of their considerable feminine wiles, lure unlucky, unwise or unwary men to their dooms."

"Am I unlucky?" wondered Nimrod. "Or am I unwise?" Aloud, he asked, "Who are you?"

It seemed at first as though she would say nothing, and he felt foolish, having asked her. Could she understand him? It seemed unlikely. Then: "Daphne," she replied, revealing again, but only for a moment, the horror that lay within her beautiful mouth. Her voice was light and tinkling, pleasing to the ear, and it cut easily through the uproar that surrounded them.

"Daphne," he said.

"Yes," she replied, making a little curtsey toward him before she turned away, as though she were embarrassed; and that was when he spied her wings. She had four of them, two pairs, and for an instant when he first saw them he thought to himself, *She's a seraph*, but then he thought, *No, the seraphim have six wings: one pair with which to cover the face, one pair with which to cover the feet, and the third pair with which to fly. And eternally they cry, Holy, holy, holy is the LORD of hosts; the whole earth is full of his glory!*

She was not an angel, could not be, not in this place where there would never be any angels. She must be an insect. But what sort of an insect was she? The dim light of pre-morning spread vivid color—red, orange, yellow, green, blue, indigo, violet—across the gleaming surface of her wings. *Like stained glass,* he thought. *Like the windows of a cathedral.* For a moment he glimpsed his own face reflected there, submerged in the shimmering colors, and he was shocked by the mixture of terror and desire he saw written on his features.

He tried, in an effort to combat the macabre welter of emotion that was rising up in him, to think clearly, categorically. They lay vertical along her back, the wings, and for a moment this fact puzzled him. She was, then, not a dragonfly—what his grandmother had called "the Devil's darning needle"—because the wings of a dragonfly do not close against its back but are horizontally outspread. What was she, then, this delicate four-winged creature that stood so demurely before him, her gaze (her eyes possessed a thousand facets, and they were set at a ghastly distance apart from each other, nearly on the sides of her head) fixed intently on his, her body turned slightly, modestly, to the side, her slender hands covering (or were they caressing?) her womanly breasts and the fuzz on her pubic mound? What was she, if not angel or dragonfly? And then—he almost snapped his fingers in relief as the thought came to him, because he, like most of us, hated almost but not quite to be able to name something—he had it: damselfly.

"Yes," she said, Daphne said, the nymph said, as though she too were relieved, as though she had somehow read his mind and realized that within him some internal struggle was over. "Damselfly." Her sibilants were thick and ungracious, as though whatever language she spoke natively did not make use of them. She took a step toward him on her slim, delicate feet, two steps, three, she was almost upon him, and her hips undulated deliciously as she walked. Her wings whirred with her excitement, throwing shards of light across the dark walls of the smokehouse, and Nimrod could feel the breeze that they made as it caressed his sweaty face. How he had wished for a breeze, back in his kitchen (it seemed like a lifetime ago, but it must have been only a few minutes, a few minutes to rise and leave his house and cross his yard and throw open the door of the smokehouse), back on the hard seat of his chair, his dogs asleep on the floor, his family resting comfortably in their beds. And now that the breeze was here...!

The wings stopped their motion, and he wanted to cry out because the breeze had stopped. The heat enveloped him again. He took a step toward her, toward the great damselfly. He thought that she must have been there with him on the battlefield, when in his delirium he had killed and killed and killed. He did not have the memory of those deaths, but she did, and she approved. She was prepared to accept him, Nimrod Nickel (*Nimrod was a great hunter before the LORD!*) as one of her own. How could he refuse such an offer? How could he possibly refuse such generosity? Her delicate face was tilted up toward his, her expression almost merry, her attitude inviting, her lissome arms outstretched.

Outside the smokehouse, the locusts went quiet. Even the numberless tent caterpillars seemed, for the moment, to have ceased their crawling. His family would miss him, Nimrod knew. His wife would sign the rich contracts (she was no fool!), and nothing could afterward stop the destruction that was coming. They would be wealthy, his wife and his son, and this place would be destroyed, and they would be far far away, in another world altogether, when the end came.

He, though—he had asked for the breeze. He had begged for it, prayed. And here it was, in these wings, in the wings of this creature that stood before him. He took her in his arms, and she was abominably light, the flesh of her lush body as unyielding as cold-rolled steel. He was shocked by the unthinkable strength of her. He was more than twice her size, a hundred times her weight, and he understood that he didn't possess even a fraction of her power. She grinned, a spectacular grin, a grin full of mandibles and palps and other damp unspeakable things. He lowered his face to hers, and she wrapped him in her fierce embrace.

Once again, the locusts took up their shrilling call. *Pharaoh pharaoh pharaoh!* they cried. On and on, endlessly.

Getting Wild with T.J. Forrester

An Interview by Sequoia Nagamatsu

T.J Forrester's stories have appeared in the *Mississippi Review, The Potomac Review, Storyglossia, Harpur Palate, The Literary Review*, and other publications. His debut novel, *Miracles Inc.* (Simon & Schuster), was released last summer and his novel-in-stories, *Black Heart on the Appalachian Trail* (Simon & Schuster) will be available this coming summer. We talk about his varied work history, his books, and his journey in becoming a writer.

SN: We've been acquaintances via *Zoetrope* for a while now, and as such, I've been able to see some of the highlights that you shared with the community in terms of your development; story publications, your search for an agent, your book deal with Simon & Schuster. But what I've always been curious about is how you got started. You've been a fisherman, a miner, a subsistence farmer, a bouncer, a construction worker to name just a few occupations. And, of course, there's your avid hiking/ outdoor background on the Appalachian trail among other places. When did you start writing? What brought you to the decision that this was something you wanted to do seriously? And how do you think your varied background has played a role in your development and identity as a writer?

Sequoia, thanks for the invitation to interview. I appreciate the opportunity to share my experiences with your readers.

I started writing in 2000, had this brilliant idea of turning my Triple Crown thru-hikes into words that magically turned into money. I was forty-five. The manuscript sucked, especially after I read Tom Robbins and was so enamored with similes I stuck them to the pages like, well...chewed Juicy Fruit. Hundreds of shitty similes, maybe millions, cluttered that work. I have no idea why it didn't sell.

Not sure I have an answer to why I kept writing, think it might have something to do with a stubborn nature. That or maybe I was delusional. I do know I fell in love with fiction, will write for the rest of my life regardless of publishing success. There is something about creating characters that makes me feel good inside. Happiness. I found it at the keyboard.

How do I think my varied background played a role in my development and identity as a writer? I am so entwined with my manuscripts that I suspect I lack the perspective to answer this question. Perhaps my diverse lifestyle opened my mind—gave me new ways of seeing the world—and that somehow translates into my fiction. I don't really know.

SN: How do you think online communities (especially *Zoetrope*) have helped in your development and current success?

Without *Zoetrope*, where I workshopped stories with scores of talented writers, I'd still be writing sentences like:

His laughter soared upward like a runaway balloon and sailed among the tittering tree branches.

SN: Your debut novel, *Miracles Inc.* follows the autobiography of Vernon L. Oliver, an alumnus of the faith healing industry, as told from his death row prison cell. First

off, let me congratulate you again on a job well done. From the first pages, your protagonist is so well crafted, a decent man accepting the wrongs he has done, reflecting on what brought him to this place. He is a man contemplative about what faith and God mean while still providing a particular kind of faith for his followers. Where did the characters and the world of *Miracles Inc.* come from? And when did you decide that this was a story that you needed to tell?

Thank you for the kind words, Sequoia.

Fiction writing, least for me, is so mysterious I gave up trying to appear intelligent when discussing the process. Basically I open my laptop, inch out until my toes hang over the cliff, then leap off the mountain not knowing if my parachute will open. What follows is so frenzied, it's all my fingers can do to keep up. God, I love that feeling. Subsequent drafts are much more controlled and tend to focus on craft. Somehow, between the beginning and the end, characters develop and stories are told.

I don't remember making a conscious decision to write *Miracles, Inc.*, stopped and started for several years, never created a compelling enough voice to carry the story. When my agent told me she needed a novel partial to sub with my collection, I sent what I had, and she sent it back saying the story was cliched. Which is a nice way of saying the manuscript was total crap. I started again, wrote eighty pages that I thought were just as totally crappy, booted the manuscript to the recycle bin, then loaded my pistol and tried to shoot myself in the head. Okay, maybe not the head, maybe I tried to shoot myself in the foot, can't remember exactly, was too drunk to aim. Hell, far as that goes, I might have loaded the spatula instead, which might explain the grease stains on what were a favorite pair of socks.

Not long afterward, I decided to throw out everything

I knew about the novel and start again. That's when I realized *Miracles, Inc.* begins after the bad thing happens. Once I made that leap, the main character came to life from sentence one, and I never looked back.

SN: Many writers begin with short stories, and the transition to novel writing can seem daunting. Can you tell me a little bit about your process and journey? Did certain writers/ books help you more than others? What was your schedule like? And what is a piece of advice you have for writers working on first novels?

My fiction writing began with short stories, and I eventually came to see them as narratives compressed into bubbles. Roundness, that's what I sense when I read a good short story. I wrote in the genre for five or so years, then decided to attempt a novel. The transition is daunting, especially when you realize you're still writing short stories instead of novel chapters, but sooner or later you adapt your storytelling to the longer narrative. Even then, writing toward a faraway unknown is scary. A novelist must trust himself, more so than a short story writer.

I learned to write short stories while studying masters like Flannery O'Connor and Raymond Carver, picked up craft advice from a number of books including Janet Burroway's *Writing Fiction: A Guide to Narrative Craft* and Sol Stein's *Stein on Writing*. Stein's book focuses on the practical, and I recommend it to writers who want a career. (The chapter on dialogue is the best I've read anywhere.)

A piece of advice for writers working on first novels? Engage the reader!

SN: Your novel-in-stories, *Black Heart on the*

Appalachian Trail, is forthcoming this summer also from Simon and Schuster. What can you tell us about this piece? And how did you go about writing the stories? Did you already have the threads that would connect the stories in mind from the get go or did you think about linking the stories together further along?

Black Heart on the Appalachian Trail was originally a collection of independent stories I began in 2005. In 2008, I revised the stories so they each linked to the AT, then secured an agent who made the sale. After signing the contract, I decided to turn the manuscript into a novel-in-stories, spent seven months developing a theme, a forward moving plot, and three character arcs. I took out two stories, wrote several more, then sent the manuscript to my editor. She acquired a linked collection, not a novel-in-stories, so I had no idea how she would receive the work. Fortunately, she loved it.

SN: Between the two books, which did you find more challenging and why?

Both books went through so many drafts and ended so differently from where they began that I can't point to one being more challenging than the other. Writing is hard. Doubt that will ever change on my end.

SN: Are you working on anything in particular now?

I'm writing content for a publishing model that targets a specific technology. Can't say more at this time.

Orange

The swirling light of a setting sun
Turns every pip of summer
Into a halfmoon-shaped dreamer

Dreaming
About a full and golden wheel
Keep running towards another season

Wrapped within the rind are ten fleshy carpels
Ten thousand juicy associations

A Puti Poem: Self-Meditating

Imagine
Sitting under a tall pipal
On a vast stretch of prairies
Where you transform your entire selfhood
Into the little marigold in front of you
Then, the running stream water
The gliding bird
The drifting cloud
The morning light
The summer sky
Where you are
The universe
Where the universe
Is you

Beasts: A Parallel Poem

Flying between sea and sky
Between day and night
Amid heavenly or oceanic blue
I lost all my references
To any timed space
Or a localized time
Except the non-stop snorting
Of a stranger neighbor

Then, beyond the snorts rising here
And more glooming there
I see tigers, lions, leopards
And other kinds of hanger-throated predators
Darting out of every passenger's heart
Running amuck around us
As if released from a huge cage
As if in a dreamland

Bearing

The purified thing streams out in a puddle,
golden and reddened in the sun.
And here is work to be done, a language
to learn, a pit bull to be taught to eat,
a hot spot flagging his mouth
with a silver dollar of crust and blood.
The needle falls from over half to empty
like a limb drifting down through water
in a long dream, but the sun is just up
and there is the hill to climb
with all its curves, Queen City
Avenue, that takes us away
from the river and toward home.
The policeman is there, he always is,
the dawn shift changing, beside
the abandoned public
swimming pool, the burnt staircase
just above the city library
rising into brush and pines.
The line has ruptured, and the fuel
must be pouring itself out like water
as I drive, but the smell and the flame
I expect do not come, or have not.
It's just an ordinary day it seems.
Over the thick red German china
I squeeze grapefruit juice
from halved rinds into my mouth.
I have it instead of coffee.
I am in pain, but so are you.

Jessica Hahn

Passing Through? One Woman's Experience Squatting in America

I had a friend who once lived in an abandoned building on Howard Street in San Francisco back in the 1990s, and she claimed there was a tunnel connecting her building to another abandoned building on Mission Street, a quarter mile down the way. I never saw that dark, black hole but another friend, at a different time, confirmed there was a passageway under the city streets where the 14 Mission bus rumbled overhead. Another friend described a network of tunnels in St. Louis, so dark no flashlight could sufficiently illuminate them, where C.H.U.D.-like people lived. My claustrophobic heart pounds at the thought of those underground scenes. I've explored utility tunnels under the campus at Berkeley, leading from manholes through tunnels and into buildings, but the closest I've come to seeing what underground homes are like has been through documentary films like *Dark Days*, and books like Jennifer Toth's *The Mole People: Life in the Tunnels Beneath New York City*. My living and sleeping quarters, although equally abandoned, have been on terra firma.

I believe that once you've walked through some dark passage, above or below ground, one's perception changes forever. The mind actively wonders about what's behind every rusty, barred door, like a growing vegetable tendril on a time-lapse camera. After exploring catacombs and tunnels and sewers beneath Paris, Neil Shea wrote of being on the surface streets and seeing a manhole: "My mind moves along that passage, imagining its path and its many branches...You picture the cool, still freedom of the underground, with all its possibilities." In my urban meanderings, lazy as a slow song, I mindlessly tromp over manholes for the most part, but put an abandoned building in my line of sight, and my mind changes it tune, and my heartbeat quickens.

Squatting has always fascinated me—the act of taking a

space, an empty place, and making it into a home, albeit temporary. The abandoned buildings are puzzling entities whose owners have disappeared into some misty bureaucratic jungle, a Bermuda Triangle of financial or physical hardship, or so it seems. When it comes to saying who owns any land, it can be argued history is a series of episodes of people claiming ownership through force (see Henry Percy, American Thinker, 2010). Squatting might be seen as taking something by force. The concept of adverse possession means, essentially, that if you squat in un-occupied place long enough, you may own the place.

In earlier days of the United States, when the people of our country were frenzied with Western expansion and Manifest Destiny, they were encouraged to seek homes by settling whatever unclaimed land tickled their fancy. The Preemption Act of 1841 encouraged men over twenty-one and widows to find up to 160 acres, squat it for a relatively short chunk of time, and purchase it from the government for as paltry a sum as $1.25 an acre before the land was publically auctioned. Congress knew people were invariably going to squat the land of this vast country, so they devised this act to make the squatters pay. On May 20, 1862, Abraham Lincoln's signature put the Homestead Act into effect, which was similar to the Preemption Act, but it also granted land ownership to freed slaves, immigrants intending to become citizens, and anyone who had never taken up arms against the American government. All one had to do was squat some acreage for five years, and pay a nominal filing fee. It's no surprise that there were thousands upon thousands of homesteaders by the end of the nineteenth century. One might say our country was founded by squatters.

Kids of the Black Hole

Some say squatting is a crime, a conflict between owner and occupier, but I think it's more of an urban lifestyle. It's about moving in a different economy, and living under the radar. More than with any other socio-political group, I associate squatting with Punk culture.

In the 1990s, when I was fifteen to twenty-five, Punk

philosophy was radical and appealing, its participants against monoculture, sexism, gentrification, the military-industrial complex, and a money-based economy. I associated Punks with squatting because they did it. They believed in direct action, whereas the academics in my schools just talked about change. Cultural theorist and historian Michel de Certeau believed that in the city "the dweller always succeeds in creating places of withdrawal, itineraries for his or her use and pleasure that are individual marks that the dweller alone inscribes on urban space." That is exactly what the squatter does, create a home in something that was abandoned, inscribe a space.

I first heard about living free when I was a teen hanging out with Punks, who, like "the kids of the black hole" in the Adolescents song, lived in the "house that belonged to all the homeless kids." They spoke of fraternity, freedom, and fun. (In the 1970s my mom and older sister lived in an abandoned shack in Central America, but their lifestyle was different than the concept of urbanized squatting that attracted me as a teenager.) Squatting was subversive, isolated from mainstream society, a "fuck you" to the structure of renting and working. And squatting seemed a viable means for a home—there were organized squats all over the world. Just look at the Lower East Side in New York City, or Christiania in Copenhagen. Laws regarding trespassing and property interpretation vary; apathetic owners, undisturbed neighbors, and, most of all, dedicated dwellers can keep the life of a squat going for quite a while.

San Francisco was in a state of flux during this time, in relation to housing availability and affordability. Erick Lyle recalled the days of the dot com boom , and in particular the gentrification of the Mission, a working-class neighborhood: "...the Mission was changing. ...the Mission's turd-and-graffiti motif was now fashionable" to the young yuppies moving in on the silicon tidal wave; plus, landlords used "...a secret weapon, a little-known California state law called the Ellis Act...to evict their tenants if they're taking the property off the rental market forever." Evictions were so common, rental prospects seemed shaky at best. Squatting was one solution, for some people, to the housing problem.

An abandoned house, like an empty city, is useless without

people—people make the home, bring it to life, define it by existing within it. Michel de Certeau wrote about people of the city, "ordinary practitioners of the city...they are walkers, Wandersmanner, whose bodies follow the thicks and thins of an urban 'text' they write without being able to read it. These practitioners make use of spaces that cannot be seen." Punks embrace the ugly, even those ugly spaces with CAUTION tape across the entrances and boards on the windows, and like urban warriors, fight for making use of those precious spaces.

Up Yours

Not only did Punks live free, but they espoused feminist ideology. Punk women embodied the antithesis of the typical standard of beauty, and Punk's lyrical respect for people who fought against sexism was impressive. (Poly Styrene, the teenage singer of X-Ray Spexs, hollering "Some people think that little girls should be seen and not heard, but I say oh bondage, up yours!" comes to mind, as does Eve Libertine of Crass singing about "shaved women collaborators" and women who are "sweet, defenseless, golden-eyed, a gift of gods repression," and Bad Brains singing "I don't want you to come to me as a whore. / Don't lust off my body baby, that's a bore.") According to Craig O'Hara in *The Philosophy of Punk*, "There is no denying sexism exists within the Punk community, but it is on a smaller level than in the mainstream, and more importantly, it is discouraged and condemned by many active participants." Squatting was not gender-biased—men and women opened buildings and lived in them.

Other role models outside of the Punk community made me think squatting was justifiable and doable, especially because I was a woman. Emma Goldman's *Living My Life* had a prominent place on my bookshelf. "I did not believe that a Cause which stood for a beautiful ideal, for anarchism, for release and freedom from convention and prejudice, should demand the denial of life and joy," she wrote. "I insisted that our Cause could not expect me to become a nun and that the movement would not be turned into a cloister." Also significant was Starhawk's *The Spiral Dance*, a modern pagan manual of sorts. She discussed the concept of a Goddess who "does not legitimize the rule of either sex by the other and lends no authority to rulers of temporal hierarchies," as well as the autonomous belief to do as you will, as long as it harms none. She was as Anarchistic as any Punk, and her spirituality was particularly affirming for females. Squatting was a real possibility.

For years the Pogues's version of "Waltzing Matilda" played in my mind: "When I was a young man I carried my pack / And I lived the free life of a rover." If that boy could do it, well so could I.

Inscribing Spaces

Although I'd explored some abandoned buildings for fun with other kids when I was kid growing up in San Francisco, the first time I slept in a squat was during my senior year of high school. I was a troubled teen without a father. My mother recently came out of jail for the felony crime of growing marijuana. I was half academic, earning good grades, and half troublemaker (fist fighting, drug taking, and an acquaintance with 850 Bryant, the local jail, for shoplifting—a charge that was dropped, I must say, because my accomplice Genevieve's mother worked as a secretary for the DA).

I visited New Orleans on the pretext of touring Tulane during my senior year. I'd been accepted, but before I committed, I wanted to see what the city was like. I had a key to one of the Pontalba Apartments on Jackson Square, courtesy of one of my mother's friends, an eclectic, artistic hippie who happened to be out of town. New Orleans was amazing—the rich food, the soulful music, the balmy air, people greeting one another. I dutifully toured Tulane, but hung out in the French Quarter every other moment.

One night, after meeting an amiable Vietnam vet in Jackson Square, I floated on Percocet down to the Moonwalk, the strip of land along the Mississippi, where a group of squatters were hanging out. I went home with them to their squat, a decrepit house a half an hour's walk away. Someone lit candles. A dragon's hoard of Mardi Gras beads hung everywhere and lay in piles, sparkling like jewels in the flickering light. My friends and I talked and drank and laughed all night until we fell asleep. I was smitten—life would never be the same. Tulane, no; abandoned buildings, yes.

Travelers in an Antique Land

Human buildings will not last till the end of time—far from it. For all the might and money behind Las Vegas and its structures that are an affront to a desert land, its black pyramid, its golden Trump tower and every ritzy, glitzy structure in between is doomed, one day. The image of ivy clambering over an abandoned pavilion is beautiful and emotional in the way that "Ozymandias," by Percy Bysshe Shelley, is beautiful and emotional:

> Two vast and trunkless legs of stone
> Stand in the desert. Near them, on the sand,
> Half sunk, a shattered visage lies...
> And on the pedestal these words appear:
> "My name is Ozymandias, king of kings:
> Look on my works, ye Mighty, and despair!"
> Nothing beside remains. Round the decay
> Of that colossal wreck, boundless and bare
> The lone and level sands stretch far away.

More far-reaching than the realm of Ozymandias is the sand on which his statue lays wrecked. In ruined Detroit with some of its fabulous old buildings, those with wood paneling carved into filigree shapes and brightly painted ceilings in cavernous lobbies, I see Ozymandias's shadow. Perhaps one of the most interesting aspects of squatting to me is the sense of time travel. It's amazing how quickly Mother Nature stakes her claim over human endeavors at immortality—look at grassy WWII autobahns in Poland, the rusty rollercoaster tracks of Takakanonuma Park in Japan, or even Sutro Baths of San Francisco, where without imagination you'd never believe vast glass swimming pools once perched on the edge of the sea. Time is humbling, so as Janis Joplin said, you better get it while you can.

I've squatted former homes, a mansion, a clinic (that still had voluminous files about patients that'd turn any stomach), and various drafty warehouses. There was printing press in Portland with running water and electricity, and a treasure chest of wooden racks filled with antique metal letters. If I wasn't so bent on traveling lightly, I'd have filled my pockets with the letters of the alphabet. Friends have told me about temporary homes in similar places, but also abandoned missile silos, subway tunnels, churches, hospitals, railway depots, under and inside of bridges, and whole neighborhoods turned into ghost towns.

The Gold Medal Flour factory of the Twin Cities is a vast place where, back in the late 1800s, they milled enough flour for twelve million loaves of bread a day—until a spark ignited flour dust and the place exploded. It was rebuilt, but then fire destroyed it. By the time I slept there, it was an eerie wreck of high, grey walls, multiple stories, and exposed staircases. I slept there in the dust, and when it rained it was more like a paste, and despite the filth, I had tender, lovely moments. If anyone thinks it's not romantic to stargaze on a balmy summer night from a rooftop vantage point, surrounded by rubble and nobody but you and yours, then I don't know what romance is.

I've been acquainted with a spectrum of floors—mushy carpets, linoleum, wood planks, concrete slabs—and used many a slice of cardboard as a mattress. I slept in places in pristine condition, homes on the market, like this one jewel box of a Victorian in San Francisco's Haight-Ashbury neighborhood. And I've slept in soggy, forlorn places, like a ruined theater in New Orleans where fliers for a performance by Grace Jones lay alongside the shellacked head of a baby alligator, the latter still in my treasure chest of odd possessions. I've mostly made my illegal beds in forgotten parts of the United States, but also in Germany (in a trashed office building) and Switzerland (at a demolition site where I woke to a wrecking ball outside the door).

On a world level, squats are about subsistence. The abandoned buildings in first world countries are luxurious by world standards, when I think of miles of shantytowns ringing the old Bombay I saw as a twelve-year-old, traveling on a shoestring with my hippie mother. Robert Neuwirth, author of *Shadow Cities*, describes Brazilian "squatter villages" of "150,000 people strong"—

I've never experienced living in an environment like that. Poverty in America is not poverty in Ghana. According to Henry Percy in *American Thinker,* "We have 35 million people living below the official poverty line, yet the average American poor person lives in 430 ft^2 of living space, again more than any Europeans except the Norwegians." (Arguably the European social programs are the better deal.) Since the big bursting of the real estate bubble in 2006, and the economic meltdown of the world economy in 2008, I notice more abandoned buildings in San Francisco than I have in years—and to walk down Market Street, the city's main street, is to see a ghost town of former businesses that crumbled long before the current decade.

In my early twenties, I was ashamed of the fact that my mother built her own house in San Francisco. After I began hopping freight trains and living in abandoned buildings, I was aware that my situation was flexible, unlike that of someone from, say, an abusive home, or addicted to drugs or alcohol. Detestable as it is, there was also white privilege at play, a reality in racist America. If I dared question how racist America was, I'd get an earful from my big sister, whose father was African-American, or from our mother who fought for Civil Rights in the 1960s. I encountered several police officers and property owners when I was squatting, and who can really say if it was because I was white, or female, or friendly, or none of the above, that caused them to give me free passage. Once was I taken to jail for trespassing, and even then the arresting officer told me, with a shameful look, that he had to because he was training his rookie partner.

My experience squatting has been positive, as has most of my travel by hook or by crook. There are many stories about squatters who've dealt with violence, addictions, and just abject situations, but they're not my story. Someone once described my mom as a Pollyanna character, and perhaps that optimism rubbed off. My father drowned when I was in diapers, and my mother was imprisoned during my high school, so I don't hold stake in luck, good or bad. A friend once chastised me by saying, "Jessica, you need to evaluate your issues of abandonment." I was never abandoned. I was born on a ship to an enterprising hippie and an expat. How could I not wander?

Logistics

Being a female in an abandoned building had its moments, like the idea of sexual dimorphism making me fear random assaults with strangers, motivating me to carry weapons and squat with friends, at least with one other person. I encountered many homeless men in my travels, but there were many women I shared a squat with. Carrying weapons meant harboring fear at some level (ironically all instances of violence in my life occurred outside of abandoned buildings). Though I was ready to run or fight if need be, my mind didn't linger in dark fantasies for longer than a few minutes. Reality was simple: food, water, and shelter.

On a logistical level, squatting had some particularly intense aspects for my gender. Having my menstrual period was a challenge in terms of cleanliness, or feeling physically capable of running away should there be a necessity to quickly evacuate. Since rusty, waterless taps were the norm, I hauled water in bottles and sometimes carried baby wipes. When I had my period, I might use pads, but socks from secondhand stores worked too. Like any creature, my friends and I didn't like to soil our homes, so we made jerry-rigged toilets out of buckets or whatever we could find, but I must admit my excrement hasn't seen the inside of several city sewers.

Another gender-related issue was pregnancy. I wanted to have a kid one day—I can be quoted as once saying, "When I have a baby I'll take it train hopping!" or some such. And when I became pregnant as a squatter, I couldn't imagine raising my child in a situation where Child Protective Services could take him or her away. I'd kill the cop who tried to steal my baby, and so I'd kill myself. Come to think of it, I couldn't imagine raising a child, period, when it was enough work just keeping myself safe and healthy.

I was never in disguise as a man, but just a young woman living my life. I accomplished my daily goal by living stealthily, dressing in black, walking confidently, talking unafraid, carrying a knife and pepper spray, or homemade weapons like a "smiley" (a padlock on the end of a bandana). I loved the feeling of living free, of waking up in a new place, of bartering instead of exchanging traditional currency, of traveling like any rugged vagabond. These are things that any squatter can do, male or female.

Whenever I opened a squat, my first task was to explore the house, and my second was to secure it. I found at least one room that could somehow be locked or barricaded, at best. My third task was checking for functional amenities. Some places had the fortune of running water, electricity, and clean carpeting. Other places moldered from decades of decay, or existed in blackened crumbling states from ancient fires—in those places, each step and footfall was carefully taken; if I had to go pee in the middle of the night, I'd tinkle in a jug rather than pad around on creaking, faulty floor boards.

Always the most important thing was being in a place where I was content to sleep—dirt and grime just didn't matter. Showers weren't an option, but safety was. I tried to create a sense of home wherever I roosted, schlepping in furniture from the street, stockpiling food, and not unnecessarily breaking things. I have done a fair share of doodling on walls with a sharpie, and once when I was in an abandoned Mercedes-Benz showroom with wall-to-wall mirrors, I hurled a heavy ashtray in a delinquent moment, just to hear the tremendous sound, like wicked wind chimes, of breaking a glassy wall. Mostly I made a home, albeit temporary, feeling safe enough to cook, kick back and relax, have sex, take naps, sleep in like a teenager on a Saturday, and of course remove my socks and boots before falling asleep.

City by the Bay

Despite being a tightly packed city, seven-by-seven miles more or less of peninsular life, San Francisco has had its flux of abandoned buildings. The first to come to mind is there no more, a gorgeous mansion up near Twin Peaks. I remember a large blackened ballroom, and a tower with a three hundred and sixty-five degree view of the city. Other abandoned buildings that come to mind are the greenhouses in the Portola neighborhood, the Naval shipyard of Hunters Point, and the MUNI bus yard on the edge of the bay.

Dan, an ex-boyfriend, and I discovered an abandoned house on Shotwell Street in San Francisco in 1996 or 1997 that we scoped out for a week, and after observing no coming or going by anyone else, we decided to open it. The house could be described as an Italianate Victorian, but was quite dilapidated. That could happen after a hundred years of use and abuse. It was rectangular, tall and narrow, two stories, an elegant composition with bay windows, balustrades in the stairway, incised decorations in the wood trim. What fool had left this to the rats and weevils? Like most of the abandoned buildings I've encountered, nobody else resided there, no winos, junkies, crackheads, or inquisitive kids. There was an empty lot next door, so one night we hopped the fence and ventured through the foxtails and six-foot-tall fennel to find a window that could be jimmied open with Dan's crowbar. I was nervous someone would catch us, but nobody did.

We ended up changing the lock on the front door, moving in our sleeping bags, some odds and ends that we had stored at my uncle's house up on Potrero Hill, and made duplicates of the keys for a buck or so on Mission Street. Being social creatures, we invited a few friends who were young and homeless, or voluntarily poverty-struck. By chance, one of our neighbors happened to volunteer at Food Not Bombs, and had a crush on one of the fellows in the squat, so he'd lug over a bucket of water every day to flush our otherwise broken toilet. About six of us lived in the house for a few months in the early spring of 1997, using candles at night, cooking food on Sternos, growing fraternal, occasionally argumentative. One day Dan and I decided to go to Mexico on bicycles. Two weeks later we were pedaling down Highway 1, laden with home-stitched panniers and definitely not wearing helmets. We were the archetypal fool, young and skipping on the cliff edge, the barking call of reason like a lapdog in our wake. We slept on precarious escarpments, and both of us missed our abandoned houses.

Live Free, NYC

I was on the Lower East Side during the summer of 1996, having hopped freight trains across country, first with two activist Punk women from Oakland to Minneapolis, and then with two seventeen-year-old boys, drunk gutterpunks, from Chicago to New Jersey. Squats in Manhattan there were remarkably different from those in California: New Yorkers had mad love, a fierce pride, and a real sense of ownership in their buildings. Their squats were like apartment buildings filled with people of all nationalities and artistic temperaments, living under one roof in a money-free economy. And the squats seemed to be equipped with modern conveniences and amenities, such as electricity and plumping that had been wrestled from the city government. They had a militant feel, much different from the laid-back California squats that I stayed in, and justifiably so—these New Yorkers were organized community members who used terms like "adverse possession," not Punks like us who were simply passing through. One couldn't just knock on the door and expect a free place to stay.

I respected the New York squats, but found them intimidating, almost like fortresses. The people living in them were homebuilders, fixing what was rotten, pouring cement, and even raising their children. Some of them didn't call themselves squatters, because "It connotes somebody who just claimed the land and did nothing but lower the value. A homesteader spent years building it up and improving it," said one resident.

One day a young man from C Squat offered to share his bed with me. Was my inroad to a coveted squat simply being a woman and a potential good fuck? It seemed to be the case. I hung out inside for a while, and despite all the political art on the walls, the practical functionality of the squat, and its organized dwellers, I was reminded of the cooperative housing structure that I ran away from two years earlier. Sascha Dubrul, a friend I met in a freight train yard, and author of *Carnival of Chaos*, wrote about a power structure in a group (not of squatters per se, but just a group of people living and producing together) that resonated with my feelings at the time: "Even in the most militantly anti-authoritarian anarchist group, there's always going to be subtle hierarchies and leaders and followers and all that nasty shit."

I chose to sleep in the East River Park with my traveling companions, the two seventeen-year-olds. A New York squatter asked me, "Why are you hanging around with boys when you can have a man?" I wasn't looking for group acceptance or a special man, just camaraderie. I'd rather be exposed to the elements, wake up with dew on my face and have cars honking in my ears, than leave my friends.

Some time later, I heard about then-Mayor Giuliani's crackdown on the people who lived and breathed by the motto "live free." It was like a war zone in the name of home ownership, abandonment, and reclamation versus law enforcement. In 1999, Michael Cooper of *The New York Times* described one scene:

Using sledgehammers, jackhammers and power saws, New York City police officers evicted a small group of heavily barricaded people yesterday from one of the few remaining tenements in the East Village still occupied by squatters.

As a police helicopter circled overhead, officers from the Emergency Service Unit wearing white sanitary-protection suits struggled to break through barricades at the front of the six-story tenement at 713 East Ninth Street, where squatters had fortified themselves behind new concrete block walls reinforced with steel.

No matter what personal issues I had with one individual in a Lower East Side squat, it would be terrible to lose what those organized homesteaders and champions stood for. In 2002, "the city sold 11 buildings on the Lower East Side for $1 each to a nonprofit agency, which [would] hand them over to the 236 squatters… The Urban Homesteading Assistance Board, which arranged the ownership transfer, is negotiating capital-improvement loans [which] will then be passed on to the one-time squatters, who will become owners of the cooperative housing. This also means the residents of each apartment will pay around $450 a month. For many, it will be the first time they have paid rent in years, though some have poured thousands of hours and dollars into making needed building repairs, such as pouring concrete staircases and patching floors and roofs." I haven't returned to New York, or know what happened with those squats, but I hope they're still going strong. More power to the people.

Conclusion

I'm a loner with a good streak of misanthropist, despite what my friends might think, and I often find nothing better than being in the absence of others, especially in the middle of a city— but I'm not in a vacuum and people mean my world.

In the late 1990s my mother got cancer and I, confronted with the possibility of being truly alone on this planet, set my compass—it led me to California on a helter-skelter course, crash-landing me in San Francisco, once again. In the many years my mother battled cancer, knocking it into remission, I missed squatting very much, but I chose to live close to her, literally in the garage of my childhood home, a sad ending to a glorious experience of freewheeling around the States. Life unfolded in unexpected ways and I became a teacher in a public school. I detested renting, and the landlords who gave me guff, and kept wondering, what really constitutes home.

Each squat I passed through was a home, but also a living museum, a testament to a sordid or dreadfully sad past, a mortgage gone belly up, or two wires crossed in a way that starts a conflagration. I love exploring abandoned buildings, every room, staircase, hallway, attic, and basement. I savor the views of alleys and brown front lawns, and the cooing of doves or pigeons in the belfry. My only regret is dealing with lingering bronchial issues and wondering if the particleboard above my head in many of those squatted buildings rained asbestos dust while I slept. I love the souvenirs from the places I stayed, a random key, a curling photograph of a stranger, the lives that were housed there before me. If a house could have a personality and a life, I imagined the abandoned houses must appreciate the occasional visitor.

Now, in my mid-thirties, I'm a mother and (egads!) a homeowner—literally, a homebuilder. The physical room in which I typed this essay was once a square of dirt in an oft-ignored neighborhood of San Francisco called Visitacion Valley, but after a year of negotiations with the city's planning department, they granted me access to construct a small home. Although it looks like a tiny ship or a Germutlicht cabin, I leave it regularly, and can often be found walking to a hilltop with a baby on my back. My eye and brain notices abandoned buildings along my route, my body reacting and brain whirring as I imagine the interior. "Places are fragmentary and inward-turning histories," wrote de Certeau, "pasts that others are not allowed to read...symbolizations encysted in the pain or pleasure of the body." This city has become my body, my footsteps encircling its boundaries, and these homes and skyscrapers and parks everywhere are all of ours as we walk, negotiate pathways, create spaces for ourselves. It excites me. There's also a lesson, part Ozymandias, part hardhat. There is definitely something to be learned from the squatter ideology. I hope to teach my daughter the cooperative values and survival skills that those C Squat parents must have taught their young, if not with lesson plans then through direct action, even if she grows up in a home that the bank owns.

Who really owns the land? We are a funny breed, us humans. One can own land, then die and pass it on, in a succession of lives and deaths of humans. We hope we're so important, writing our memoirs or polemical tracts, but in the advent of global warming life as we know it might (de)volve to a far more practical, subsistent, hand-to-mouth venture. My life partner is a person of science, and he tells me that even if the nuclear bombs went off, and all humans died, the only things to remain would be the oceans, lower forms of life, and the land. Eventually plants and animals would come back. Trees grow, roots deepen, streams change their course, and homes are built by muscles. We kill for the land that we think we own. In all reality, we are passing through, on a temporary basis, and in the meantime we are caretakers.

My Aunt Yola

Aunt Yola let her white neglige slip to the floor.

Steve and I had never seen a woman nude before. She was a big lady, a huge, fat cow of a woman, and Uncle Bob had been asleep for hours at that point. And she motioned for us to follow her, but I didn't know what to do. Steve moved forward. Aunt Yola placed a stale donut in a napkin and left it on the TV tray. She said that it was for me, and it was okay to be scared because the brave were ignorant.

She took Steve into the dimly lit bedroom and shut the door behind them. I sat in the living room for some time. Uncle Bob was still asleep on the couch, the funny papers bunched up under his bare legs and his big slab of an arm draped over his eyes. He breathed deep and loudly. I didn't eat the donut.

The light switched off in the bedroom.

My father had sent us across the street that night with two eggs, one for myself and the other for Steve. But we never got to eat them. I wandered into the kitchen and drank out of a coffee pot. The milk in the fridge had gone bad, and I remember having diarrhea earlier that day. I wanted to know what Steve was doing, but I wouldn't go near the door. Instead, I went back into the family room and alternated looking at Uncle Bob's heaving gut and blankly staring into the television screen, long gone into static.

Shortly after, I heard the metal knob on the door jiggle and Steve walked out, gingerly. Aunt Yola was on her stomach, lying naked on the bed. Steve and I lied down on the den floor together.

He was sad, and would be turning twelve the next day.

Silver Belly of a Rockfish

When Owen Baugher and his sister Elsie were ten and seven respectively, Aunt Ginny took them to Dewey Beach, Delaware, for a single week in August. The Baughers lived in a small town in western Maryland, a town so small that there were three acceptable ways of pronouncing its name. Tricia Baugher, Elsie and Owen's mother, ran a small farm year-round, but most of the profit stemmed from the holiday season and the adjoining farm-fresh restaurant she opened just last year.

"My sister, she's got the business sense," Aunt Ginny said to the weekend customers. She wiped down the display tables with a white cloth and stacked them again with jars of raspberry jam and peach preserves. "I'm the sassafras," she'd add. "I tease the customers and show a little leg." Then Aunt Ginny would step a toe out and give a twist. Often found stretching her lithe runner's muscles, hands clasped behind her back or swinging her arms while perfecting a flamingo pose, Aunt Ginny had trouble with stillness. Her older sister Tricia, however, dug her heels in the dirt, always had since a toddler, mesmerized by a praying mantis or standing guard near a newly acquired pet.

On a Saturday, when a pretty young girl, one with a shiny wash of hair, strolled through with her family, Aunt Ginny pinched Owen by the shoulders and warned him in a serious tone that this was his only chance for great love. "Make your move, Owen," she said and then with a sharp shove, she pushed him in the direction of the young blond thing. "You can do it, big man. Just keep it real. Show that 4-H prize-winning filly your Baugher swagger." His pudgy body bounced between the cherry pie tables as he inched toward the girl and the fresh heads of lettuce. Aunt Ginny pressed her fingertips to her mouth, shielding a smile. "Sheepish like your Mama," she said, as Owen veered toward the cucumbers and away from possibility.

When Aunt Ginny moved in three years ago, they had to make room. Elsie was to share Owen's bedroom, and together they cleared the downstairs closet—a tightening of space. But Aunt Ginny was so full of life, that Owen followed her heel-to-toe from the far edge of the apple orchard to the decrepit petting zoo (a wiry pair of guinea pigs and an irritated rabbit) beyond the parking lot. Whether applying the Baugher stickers to glass jars or refilling water troughs, Owen huffed beside his Aunt, offering his ear and an extra pair of hands; Elsie tagged along, too, her red nose chapped from allergies. She carried her pink baseball hat and filled it with fistfuls of clover to be sifted through later for luck.

Aunt Ginny told Owen secrets. She ushered him outside, near the unpainted corner of the barn, where, like a boy-crazed eighth grade girl, she twisted a long weed around her ring finger, while divulging her latest relationship woes. Elsie heard these secrets, too, but was uninterested in love. Owen listened patiently to his aunt's inner debates. He suggested she ditch the gross man who'd been phoning her lately. The name, he didn't like either, and announced that "Chuck," reminded him of throw-up. Aunt Ginny's hands gripped his, and she made him promise he wouldn't spill the beans to his mother: "Tricia dissects fun like a science project," she said. A forceful nod was Owen's way of showing how deadly serious he could be.

"I think I found one," Elsie called, picking through the green mass in her upturned cap. Her sneezes came is threes. "No. Nevermind. It's just a regular."

Aunt Ginny's announcement to take the kids for the week was met with hesitation and concern. Flour marked Tricia's cheeks, and she balled up a brown dishrag to blot the sweat from under her arms. Owen and Elsie pressed close to their mother like goats, and with clenched muscles, they promised to call three times a day. When Tricia Baugher acquiesced Owen froze and grabbed Elsie's elastic waistband in disbelief.

By Monday morning, they were packed in Aunt Ginny's boxy blue Corolla, and Owen imagined oil paintings of what he might see, thick with textured brushstrokes. He'd never been to a real beach before, the kind with rainbow umbrellas and lifeguards in high white chairs. Their mom and Aunt Ginny had been raised between the boardwalk slats, but only his aunt seemed proud of it. Behind him, in the backseat, Elsie made bracelets out of plastic string she called gimp. She wormed forward, elbows on the console, and tried to teach her brother how to make them, but Owen grew frustrated when the green plastic strips undid themselves no matter how tight he pulled.

Aunt Ginny told them stories of her teenage years on the Delaware shore. She spoke of skinny brown bodies, tan boys with white teeth who carried her on their shoulders before tossing her to the waves headfirst. There were miniature crabs that dug into the wet sand leaving as evidence a constellation of air holes, and pruned fingers coated in a salty glaze. Aunt Ginny fished above the visor for her sunglasses. She urged Owen and Elsie to roll down their windows and let the air knot their unwashed hair. "To be young," she said. "To be silly wind-up toys wound to the hilt." Owen wasn't sure he agreed; he pictured his old plastic crate filled with wind-up toys including a yellow duck, an alligator, and a boxing kangaroo that back-flipped. All were compact and stiff with lifeless eyes.

The car ride passed to the sound of Aunt Ginny's throaty tales of night swimming, the waves like wet shadows, and stolen beach souvenirs such as shot glasses and candle holders made from clamshells. In the dead heat of summer, the beach shops were swarming with lazy tourists, their sopping wet bathing suits bleeding through their cotton shorts. Weaving between sunburned knees, Aunt Ginny would gather handfuls of shells from wicker baskets and stuff them in her pockets; later she'd sell them on the beach for a dime a piece.

Aunt Ginny's bare knee caught a disc of sunlight, and Owen stared at the blue and purple veins that gathered there; a sea urchin just under the skin.

Elsie finished a green and red box-style bracelet, a stick of Christmas. She tied it to her wrist, pulling the chewy ends with her teeth.

Bare feet propped on the dash, Owen pressed his toes to the windshield, and round smudges blurred the view.

"It smells different here," Elsie said.

Aunt Ginny adjusted her grip on the wheel. "That, my little sand beetle, is the ocean."

The Southwinds Motel was turquoise blue and white with a white wooden railing that lined the stairwell and the second floor walkway. The doors were orange and Owen told Elsie that somebody forgot to paint them. "It used to be brown and orange," he said. "But when they repainted it, they ran out of blue. That's why it doesn't match."

"You don't know," Elsie said. "You've never been here." She ran back to Aunt Ginny and helped her roll the zebra striped suitcase over the gravel parking lot while Owen scattered the remains of his Fritos for the gathering gulls. Their hooked beaks stabbed at the chips, and the largest one flapped his wings with great bravado to exude dominance over the rest. When Owen ran at them with full force, they didn't explode in a flurry of wings like the robins on the farm; instead, three tall gulls hopped backwards and twisted their necks from side to side.

The room was dark, cooler than the outdoor air, and a wet smell hugged the walls. When Aunt Ginny pulled back the brown felt curtains, dust burst from the fabric folds like small puffs of cigarette smoke. There was so much sunlight outside, not a single cloud to cut the glare, but none of it crept into Room 203. The tinted windows cocooned the space and muted the orange wall panels that matched the orange door. Elsie unzipped the zebra suitcase and shoved an armful of pink and purple underpants in the top drawer, followed by socks she'd never wear, her strawberry bathing suit, jeans with the hearts on the back pockets, and three of Owen's old T-shirts which she liked to sleep in because each one covered her small frame like a parachute.

Owen sat on the edge of the twin bed. The other twin bed mirrored his, except it sat a few inches lower to the ground. "We don't all fit," he said to Aunt Ginny.

"Sure we do," she said, a palm tree beach towel pinned between her chin and her chest. From behind the terry cloth wall, she wriggled her swimsuit up her torso. "It's all a state of mind. Think grand."

Owen hit the old-fashioned remote, a fat rectangle with one red button. The television made a popping sound, and a black and white Western howled to life, top volume; the horse reared and two men fired, one sharp shooter tumbled backwards off his horse, his face busting the dry earth. Owen liked the Roy Rogers Westerns in color better than this old-fashioned black and white pistol flick. The movie looked fake, even the guns. Roy Rogers was an honest man and Trigger was the best horse around.

"We'll get a roll-a-way or a cot or something," said Aunt Ginny, but Owen didn't hear her over the gunshots and galloping hooves.

Outside, Elsie led the way with a sandcastle bucket, the handle looped on her forearm. Two white shovel heads clacked together as she bunny-hopped down the stairs. The yellow bucket had been hiding in the shade beneath the staircase, and Elsie had discovered it when she retrieved her pillow from the car. It was nearly new; a price tag dangled from the handle with a clear plastic ring. The Delaware summer heat stuck to Owen's white, freckled skin and Aunt Ginny reminded them both for the third time that day to call her by her first name only. It should only be "Ginny" if they see her chatting with an attractive man. "The label 'Aunt' can age a lady," she added.

"What if he's ugly?" Owen asked. "What if he's got a fat belly and loads of neck hair?" Elsie laughed a little and repeated the last part about the neck hair.

Aunt Ginny halted on the sidewalk and stretched her calves. "This heat will do us in," she said and pulled a lukewarm High Life from her canvas tote.

The beach was not near the motel, and Elsie complained of a blister between her toes right where the plastic divider of her flip-flop had rubbed away a fine layer of skin. With a slight limp, she swung her plastic bucket around and around, marveling at how the shovels stayed inside, even when the bucket was fully upside-down.

"*She sells seashells by the seashore,*" Elsie announced with rhythmic precision, conducting the air with her free hand. "*She sells seashells by the seashore.*"

Owen squinted from the sun's harsh glare and every few minutes a chalky pick-up truck or bruised hatchback would blaze by, honking and hooting with its bass lines vibrating the asphalt.

"*The shells she sells are gathered in Hell.*" Elsie, forgetting her blister, hop-scotched to the rhythm of her own voice, posing in a crude arabesque.

"Who taught you that?" Ginny asked, and smacked Elsie on her bottom.

The trio passed a few seafood shacks, a liquor store, and a bar called Gary's Surf and Spray Cafe with a sign out front jammed in the sand like a for sale" marker. It read: FREE SHOOTERS WITH PURCHASE OF POPCORN SHRIMP.

The parking lot was nearly empty except for two people: a man wearing a leather vest who straddled his low, black motorcycle, while a scrawny woman leaned against the back tire and slid her bathing suit strap off her shoulder to inspect her tan line. A head jerk, angry arms that made a T, and a voice rumbled low as she tracked them like fresh meat; the man on the bike turned, too, and as if challenging the boy, he revved the bike's engine. The low roar was charged with fat, exploding pops that filled Owen's gut and rushed to the tops of his ears. Fine sand and dust swirled around the couple, masking their feet and blurring all the parking lot lines that Owen could see.

"What are shooters?" asked Elsie.

"Little guns for killing small animals," Aunt Ginny answered, winking at Owen, who smiled back broadly, in on the joke.

"Really?" asked Elsie, looking hard between her aunt and her brother.

"Just the rodent ones, honey," Aunt Ginny said. "Rats and raccoons and opossums."

"Oh." They shuffled along the road in penetrating heat. "Okay."

"And hamsters," Owen added. "And baby rabbits." Owen snickered then.

"Stop making fun," Elsie whined and she stormed ahead, wincing as the rubber rubbed her blister raw.

The beach was cloaked in the colors of summer, and the tawny sand seared the bottoms of bare feet. Atlantic waves crashed and dissolved into a bubbling sea of white foam before the suds were sucked beneath the next blue muscle. Strings of seaweed lined the water's edge like discarded fishing nets, and two boys were whipping the ends of a limp strand against the shoulders of a squealing young girl. In the heart of the swells, a father held his toddler above the waves, fighting for his own balance as the powerful force submerged all but his hands and the bright face of the small child.

Pioneering a path between damp towels and sweating coolers, Aunt Ginny pointed to dead jellyfish sprawled in gelatinous lumps; the small ones were easy to miss, mucus balls coated with sand, but the large ones captivated Elsie, who crouched down beside each clear mound, poking at its body as if a world lived inside.

Owen let Elsie pick the spot. The packed sand was hard and damp from high tide, so most beach-goers had opted for alternate plots with loose, dry sand that would mold beneath sprawled bodies.

Off in the distance, further down the beach where fewer people chose to lie, a giant wooden spear ran the width of the beach, a squat wall of logs that skewered the water. To Elsie it was a distant balance beam. When she asked her brother what it was, he told her it was a pipe that connected Dewey Beach to Russia, that letters, old clothes, and unloved pets rolled between continents, a sort of primitive post office.

Aunt Ginny dropped her beach towel in a heap and dashed

to the ocean like a child on fire. The back of her limbs and the way in which the tendons and muscles harmonized reminded Owen of his mother—a former athlete encased within sun-spotted skin. But never had he witnessed his mother race toward anything with such fervor, with such abandon that it radiated from her backside as if she might flap her fins and soar over the whitecaps till she were nothing but the silver belly of a rockfish.

In the few hours apart from the farm, away from shelled peas, distanced from price stickers and rattan displays, Owen felt he every sense heightened. The August sun was cooking something beneath the skin. Owen's toes wriggled under clumps of wet sand shucked by his sister's plastic trowel. With great determination Elsie dug a trench, a seven-foot moat crafted to catch crabs and seashells delivered by the enemy line. Waves crashed together and shot a spray straight up, geyser-like. Owen grabbed a solitary strand of seaweed and ran a loose fist along the stem. The slick tendrils encircled his wrist, and he whipped a green figure eight in the air before he heaved the rope over his body and lashed the ground with brutal strokes, splitting the surface with shallow gashes. Instinctively, Elsie covered her face.

Tuesday, Wednesday, and Thursday progressed with a similar chain of events: the long, hot walks to the beach and the dust from passing cars made all three salivate for the chilled ocean spray. Owen had made casual friends with the brothers from a large family who also enjoyed the hard, packed sand, and Aunt Ginny discovered that a ten dollar bill would keep Owen occupied for the afternoon in search of the perfect french fries. All of their stomachs were saturated with greasy beach food and sticky soda diluted with melted ice. Elsie and Owen had sunburns across their backs and shoulders; they doused themselves in Aunt Ginny's SPF 8 lotion once in the mornings, taking turns with the small purple bottle. The motel offered a cool respite in the evenings, but there were spiders that clung to corners and dropped from the showerhead when the water sprang forth, and Elsie's bath towel had a brown stain along the edge; it sat dry and untouched on the back of the toilet. She used Aunt Ginny's wet towel instead.

At night, Elsie had trouble sleeping on her metal cot—the springs whined, she said, and the sheet smelled funny—a dirty hamper smell. The murmurs of the nighttime television dramas drowned out the loud voices outside. It was in those dark, sleepy hours that Aunt Ginny would disappear for *grown-up time*, kissing both children on the forehead—Elsie squirming away—and tucking the only key in the pocket of her white shorts.

The AC kicked on loud for ten-minute spurts, but generated more sound than cold air, and every night Owen woke at 4:00a.m. drenched in sweat. By Thursday night, the metal cough of the AC and the quiet that followed sent a heat shivers across Owen's damp skin. He unraveled himself from the coiled cord of the sheet and padded softly around the room. Something glass shattered outside, like a bottle knocked off a railing, and a car alarm scooped the air with loud whine.

Every night that week was drenched in vicious thunderstorms, the rain pounding the roof in sheets of sharp water. The mornings, though, held a new promise of fresh air and an all-day escape from the dank musk of the Southwinds Motel.

A new sign appeared every morning in front of the roadside bar that announced the day's deals, and on Friday the specials read: LADIES NIGHT! $5 MARGARITAS AND ALL-U-CAN-EAT WINGS.

"See that?" Aunt Ginny asked. "Margaritas and wings will turn a stomach inside out. You remember that, the both of you. When you're old enough to drink, you stay away from that combo platter of trouble."

Elsie marched backwards, picking up her knees to keep her to keep her flip-flops on her feet. The side door of the bar swung open, and a squat, red-faced man flung a garbage bag in the dumpster.

Elsie stopped and pointed big at Aunt Ginny. "You're trouble," she said.

"What did you say, young lady?" Aunt Ginny asked. The squat man let the dumpster lid fall with a squeal and thud.

"Mama says that. She says, 'Don't you be like your Aunt

Ginny. That one's a whole mess of trouble." Elsie swung her yellow bucket and dust rose from the gravel like smoke off a wet log.

Aunt Ginny gave a look, as if Elsie had stepped out of her own skin. She laughed a metal laugh, her silver cavities bright, and Owen drew back to make himself small.

"Well, aren't you just like your Mama. Can't help but dissect all the fun out of a day. Gotta slice open the underbelly of a dead frog." A Budweiser sign buzzed neon in the window and a streetlamp was on even in the daylight. "That's what you do!" Aunt Ginny chuckled. "You dig in there with a little toy knife."

Owen laughed, too, because Aunt Ginny was laughing and also because Elsie was not.

Elsie screwed up her face and grunted low. She charged at her aunt hard, one fist deep inside her yellow bucket like a hand in a boxing glove and jammed the plastic end full force into Aunt Ginny's lower back, which caused her to pitch forward and fall to her knees. "I hate you!" she said, her right foot stomped the ground near Aunt Ginny's hand. Elsie alternated between running in place and hopping back and forth like a tennis player. "I hate this stupid trip. The motel smells and I have to sleep on a cot. You'd never sleep on a cot. We're only staying there because you have no money. You can't even afford to buy us a real lunch. I hate hot dogs and I hate fake Coke."

"Shut up, Elsie!" Owen yelled in his sister's ear. "Guess what? Mom called and she wants you back at the farm." He extended a soft elbow to Aunt Ginny for support. Little dots of blood were swelling on her kneecaps and it reminded Owen of something from kindergarten, of a metal sifter from the sandbox or a green plastic tool that made pasta out of Play-Doh. "Look. You made her bleed," he said, and then, "Nobody signed up for a babysitting job." He waited for Aunt Ginny to agree, to chime in with her own biting remark, but her attention was lost on three pick-ups ambling by, a parade of trucks with large wheels splattered with mud. The last one slowed to crawl, the gravel popping with each revolution of the tires, and a woman with yellow hair and the complexion of baked potato skin shoved her breasts over the open passenger window.

"I said to Chuck here, Virginia 'Ginny'"Baugher is back in town, but he told me to suck his pierced nipple." She coughed out a grin. "Ain't no way in hell, he said. Called me a liar." Chomping on blue gum, this baked-potato woman looked Aunt Ginny up and down, and wheezed as she slapped the outside metal of the truck door. "Some nerve you got." The woman's face crinkled like a well-used plastic bag, and she gestured with an unlit cigarette butt, all the smoke drained through a long yellow filter. The man at the wheel didn't budge. He kept his eyes on the road, eyeing the oil patches up ahead that shimmered and rippled in the midday heat. "You steal those kids, too? Or you renting them by the hour?" she asked, then flicked the dead butt clear over Elsie's head.

Aunt Ginny stepped toward the truck and planted her feet. "Amber Dixon, the last time I saw you, Chuck had crushed your cheekbone with the doorframe. It swelled so bad, it puffed your eye shut. Healed nicely, though. Can hardly tell."

Amber shut off the truck radio. "Better me than you, right?" she said. "I turned that busted cheekbone into a ring and a joint bank account. From what I hear, a little accident like that could do you some good."

With an arm through the straps of her tote bag, Aunt Ginny hurried Owen and Elsie toward the open front door of the Gary's.

"I sent a memo!" Amber hollered. "Told all the women to lock up their men till you leave town."

Elsie turned back around, just her head over her shoulder, straining for that final glimpse of the crumpled woman, a woman who might pass for a teenager from the back, beautiful even, behind a sheer dingy drape or a frosted shower curtain. The sun, however, revealed every crack and flaw. The grip was tight on Elsie's upper arm and Aunt Ginny jerked her forward.

Amber smacked the air with an open hand and bellowed a two-toned battle cry. It reminded Owen of an old-time Indian call, the kind that soared from a chief who rode bareback, the one in the movies with the feathered headdress blown back by the wind. The truck rumbled along the shoulder until it kicked into high gear, forcing a small silver sedan to break fast and shift lanes.

There wasn't much said about Amber, but Owen saw an expression color his aunt's face, like sipping flat soda. She looked older to him and sleep-deprived. With outstretched palms, Owen and Elsie collected quarters from Aunt Ginny to play songs in the jukebox at Gary's. Elsie selected her songs based on the album's cover art, such as the fiery blue stallion that graced *Steve Miller Band's Greatest Hits*. Cross-legged, Aunt Ginny sat in the booth and sipped a Bloody Mary through a straw.

The waves at the beach that day were the most turbulent they had seen, sea creatures thrashing from the depths. The midnight thunderstorms in conjunction with high southwestern winds generated massive ocean swells that sucked panels of crushed shells into the surf and hurled them back to the shore where they were barely permitted to breathe in the open air before drawn under again. Large red flags were posted by each lifeguard stand along with harsh warnings of rough beach conditions. Red letters and multiple exclamation points.

"When you were my age, anyone dare you to swim in that?" Owen asked. Waves were breaking on top of one another, toppling like dominos.

"That's the whole goddamn point of those years. You got a lifetime to grill chicken, right bud? Decades to stand by the gas pump." She cupped his shoulder. "Not your mom, though. Barely got in up to her knees. Said the tide felt like fingers. Collected all sorts of beach crap instead to put in jars." Aunt Ginny and Owen watched Elsie skip to the water and wait with bent knees for a series of waves to thunder down. Then, she screamed as she tore away from the shoreline, waving her hands and shrieking in mock terror. "When the ocean's wild like this, it can rattle your brain. Spin you so senseless you forget which way is up."

Chunks of sand spit behind Owen as he raced Aunt Ginny to the water's edge. She darted like an insect, this way and that, arms up, her hands open like she surrendered, finally registering the mountainous form, and then gone, a needle pierced through the base of the cascading ocean wall. She couldn't help it. Once the water licked her toes, she sprinted toward the wave, launching herself clear through to the other side of something that threatened to flip her backwards, crush her flat.

But Owen followed, commanding his calves to march bravely through resistance, the knee-deep water swirling and rushing past. The distance ballooned, an elastic band that stretched and snapped, but the shore was further now. A glint, a spark of light, bounced off Aunt Ginny's back, the silver ring on her swimsuit, must have been that ring, it flared and then gone, engulfed by the giant wave that now dwarfed Owen's boyish form. They would return to shore later, eyes sore with salt sting, and Owen would ask first how far down the current had pulled them. He would ask this not recognizing their basic brown towels pulled taut, lying in perfect rectangles on the sand. But first he had to follow Aunt Ginny's lead. He sucked in a cup of air, shut his eyes and braced for the hit.

While her brother tumbled beneath the surface of greens and blues and Aunt Ginny rode the distant wave humps, Elsie's attention was fixated on land. She busied herself with her yellow bucket, the sandcastle mould she had found in the motel parking lot on their very first day. It had three spires and a central tower, much more intricate than the buckets sold in the beach shops along Coastal Highway; those only boasted one central dome and the outline of a single castle door. The whistles blew and hurt Elsie's ears, so she lugged her loaded bucket further down the beach, away from all the commotion, further down the beach toward the groyne, a fence of logs that cleaved the sea like a longsword.

It was peaceful at this end. Her strawberry bathing suit bunched at the bottom, so she stopped to pick at the wayward band with her index finger, belly out, further down the beach than she'd ventured this entire week. No families wanted to lay their towels by algae covered logs, the part of the beach where swimming was forbidden and orange buoys were tossed about like popcorn. The sand, marbled with black ribbons of varying widths, posed toxic and gritty like the greenish surge, and an afghan of seaweed, a loose knit of purple and red rode the surf. But the shells, harbored in the crooks of the wooden spur, were impeccable replicas of miniature fans. Unbroken, with all their ridges and bowtie tails. A few of these treasures were a vibrant shade of maroon, others were mottled gray and brown, but many—oh so many—were perfectly white. She would sell a few dozen to the beach shop but keep most of them for herself in a glass bowl. Clear or aquamarine.

The ground, it was level near the water, so that's where Elsie turned her sandcastle bucket upside-down, wriggling the plastic gently until the solid shape released. With a cupped palm, she scooped a few drops of water to dot the drier side and smoothed the foundation with her thumbs. The empty bucket was needed for the shells. All those perfect shells. She rescued each one and stacked three precise columns in the hollow yellow fortress. There were hundreds to save before the tide came in and nibbled little bites from her sandcastle, before the froth swam to shore and made it hard to see, made her wide eyes burn when she plunged her face below the surface, the current thrumming her sun burnt ankles, the wooden groyne a slippery splintered hand, as Elsie scoured blind for just one more.

What the Nose Knows

There was a man and he had many gifts but the chief gift was that to everyone he smelled good. It sounds like a small gift but it was not because everyone who got close enough to smell him was reminded of his or her most cherished memory. To some he smelled like the sea, to others like a forest in the rain. Some described the scent as yeasty and sweet like a bakery. Because of this people were kind no matter how he acted from the time he was very small. No one could hate him or be mean to him because to do so would defile the memory of what they held most sacred. He grew up loved through no fault of his own.

And though everyone told him how good he smelled the man could not smell himself. He wanted this more than anything and it colored his existence and kept him free from any real accomplishment. The man grew up and took a job as a salesman in a small clothing store and he was very good at this because everyone who came in felt so happy to be around him. The boutique attracted many people who came and bought things they did not need or want but returned again and again because they had such fond memories of being in the shop. The man had lots of money and lots of women but he wasn't happy. He felt as if he did not know himself. He decided to leave the shop and Claudine, a woman who cared for him. He traveled around the world but the more he saw, the emptier he felt. He stood inside the great dome of the Hagia Sophia and though people clustered around him like discreetly eager bees he felt more hollow than ever. The great beauties of the world did not move him. He began to fear that he was not a moral man although he had committed no crimes. Nothing he had ever desired had been withheld from him except this one thing, that he was lost to himself.

He decided to travel to Paris to meet with a great perfume maker who was famous for his nose and his ability to create complex scents from simple oils. The perfume maker sensed that he had a great find in the man and paid him to stay in Paris. For a year, the perfume maker and the man lived together. The perfume maker took detailed notes about how the man smelled in different conditions, when it rained, by the ocean, when he was happy. Other noses came to his chateau and sniffed, making their own notes and suggestions.

The man was lonely and he hated being studied. He could see how hard the perfume maker was working and knew that perfume maker believed this would be his magnum opus. Late at night the lights in the lab were on and deep plum shadows bloomed under the perfume maker's eyes.

The man spent much of his time in the perfume maker's large flower garden reading his books, which were mostly about horticulture. It was in the garden that he noticed a strange thing. Bees, usually so drawn to sweet things, ignored him cold. They hovered around his glass of prosecco and clustered in the flowers nearby busily packing their knees with pollen. The man could not believe that he had never noticed such a thing before. The man thought this was very important and rushed off to tell the perfume maker.

The house echoed with cool marble stillness in the full heat of midday. The man ran to the laboratory and pushed open the door. The perfume maker tinkered amidst vials and beakers. The room smelled of a war of flowers, assaultively heavy. The perfume maker had moved beyond the horticultural realm. In one beaker, champagne fizzed, in another bits of shell clattered and in the center of the room, a delicate young girl in a pale blue dress stood, her bare feet in a crystal bowl full of water.

The man was stunned. "Who is she?"

The perfume maker looked up. "That is my daughter, Gisele. I asked her mother to send her to me for a visit. To me, your scent is like when she was born and the top of her head smelled like butter and honey drizzled on warm bread."

"You can't help me." The man said with a sigh, knowing now how subjective scent truly was.

"No, no. I have done it. Try this." He thrust a small vial under the man's nose.

It stank of decay, the taste of dirty metal, and the pervasive rot of untended things. "That's disgusting." The man recoiled in horror. "I do not smell like that."

The perfume maker was baffled. "It's not sweet to you?" He held the vial out to Gisele who sniffed and smiled. "It is like bubble gum."

The man snatched the vial away. "You know nothing." He stormed out of the lab and accosted people on the property and asked them to sniff. They all reported the most heavenly scent. The man left the perfume maker disgusted. The memory of what he had smelled stayed with him. He did not remember where he knew the smell from but it was as familiar as illness. It pervaded his being until only the stink remained. It was as if his nose was submerged in it always and the sense of it etched deep lines of disgust on his face. Those who were drawn to him by his scent were soon scared off by his scowl.

Pamela Balluck

In the Briefcase Veronica Gave Me After Grace Died

1.

Grampa's wallet, made by Rolfs, god knows how many decades ago, and in it: a National Retail Credit Association card from Goodman Furniture, Cleveland, Ohio (Member Since 1920); his California driver's license, expired 1-14-89, twenty years ago, seventy-nine years after DOB, 1910 (I thought it was 1909); '75 Health Insurance card (Gramma was still alive, in San Diego); Sherman Oaks Library card; '91 Patient Lens Implant Identification Card; business card of Attorney-At-Law in Hollywood hand-updated from old 213 to new 323 area code; business card of Pac Bell Service Technician; '72-issued AARP membership card (Mom was still alive), expiration '99 (he expired '05); November '04 yellow customer copy of $10.00 Master Card receipt from Kaiser Radiology in Panorama City signed in his blindman's scrawl, without the special glasses he wouldn't wear in public, the capital J of his first name and capital G of his last name nonetheless distinct (I can picture Grace's manicured fingernail pointing out the line); Senior Discount Card from Marie Callender's on Ventura with Sylvia and phone number written in black ink on one end, in black ink on back Liza Naomi 2-19-95 (Flora passed away summer before), and upside down below it, Sharla and phone number, above that in red ink Victory & Coldwater / San Remo; business card of Washington Mutual Senior Financial Associate in Sherman Oaks; Auto Club of Southern California Emergency Road Service plastic-key card; unsigned L.A. Public Library card ("Check it out"); North Hollywood M.D.'s card, his printed info crossed out in pen and on back written, under For Emergency in Cleveland, Grampa'sbrother's name, address, and phone number in Ohio, Uncle Sam, the dentist, who Grampa outlived; in black ink on a white scrap, printed in Grace's hand,

MORNING

½ - *MICRONASE 2.5 MG*

½ - *CESTRIL 2.5 MG*

½ - *LOPRESSOR 25 MG*

1 - *COATED ASPIRIN*

1 - *PRAZOSIN 2 MG*

EVENING

1 - *MEVACOR 10 MG*

1 - *PRAZOSIN,*

faded and fuzzy at bottom, with the milligrams worn off.

2.

Grampa's Passport, issued 1983, in which his date of birth is January 19, not 14; birthplace same as mine, New York; and, past his signature, like the pages of my own Passport, blank. Where did he want to go? Where will I go and when?

3.

White manila, labeled with my name and my sister's in red pen by Grace's daughter, Veronica,containing: brown business envelope from Department of Health and Human Services dated bypost mark and in pencil July 1994, in pencil WILL, Flora-related (they married in '77), and inside Affidavit of Death of Joint Tenant from the office of the Attorney At Law in Grampa's wallet and a copy of Flora's death certificate; Grampa's death certificate, according to which he was last seen alive the day before the date on which I've been lighting candles for four years and says his parents were born in Lithuania (I thought it was Russia—I search out a map); business envelope postmarked 1960, addressed to Grampa in Cleveland, from Court House, holding a certificate in which the governor of Ohio appoints him Notary Public; 1972 Service Agreement with San Diego mortuary witnessed by Gramma (whose Service Agreement was fulfilled in '77) for Grampa to be cremated—lists Russia as his parents' birthplace; an un-postmarked brown Los Angeles Passport Office envelope addressed to Grampa at Flora's on Wonderland (before her stroke), Passport penciled in Grampa's hand on front (I place his Passport inside), then Grace's printing in black ink, MARRIAGE CERT. and my grandparents' names, a certificate that has them married in Cleveland in 1931 (Did they stomp on a glass?); a copy of Grampa's birth certificate,on which his penned-in birth date appears to be Jan, 24.

4.

Loose: computer printout of one of Grampa's corny poems about Grace—before she became his wife—the widowed next-door neighbor to the FEMA apartment he lived in for two years until his and Flora's condo, damaged by the Northridge quake, was repaired (Flora died the summer after the quake at a nursing home she'd been in for years); more poetry in pencil and in pen; printed wall flier pointing to Grampa's memorial service; two-sided, legal-sized, captioned photo collage I sent color-copies of as hand outs for the service in L.A. when I couldn't get away from Salt Lake in time, photos starting with my grandparents, young and hip in 1930, transitioning through the best of more than fifteen years with Flora, and ending with Grace at the turn of the century; printout of the three-page double-spaced remembrance narrative I sent for my sister to read aloud in place of me; handwritten card from Grampa's nieces, Sam's daughters, accompanying a paragraph they asked Grace to read aloud at the memorial; a white Holiday Inn envelope containing twelve unused, unstamped parking lot passes.

5.

A grey manila, address label peeled off, postmarked 1995: in it, more of Grampa's cheesy lovepoems to Grace.

6.

Manila manila on whose flap is jotted You are an angel in disguise / Every breath spoken brighten [sic] my skies. Grace.

Amy Schreibman Walter

The Permanence of a Polaroid

How quickly city starlings will fly away –
when they are bothered, it seems.
We eat cherries from a cracked blue cup,
watch them do a mating dance,
perform as though they know
we are seeing.
How quickly you note that birds in the city are scrawny,
that even starlings, they call for something,
and we sip tea with too much sugar,
watch their feet as they dance
like only starlings can dance -
wildly, in the dirt.

Guidelines of Rose Gardens

He ran behind my dreams
as a tornado of geraniums
and glass, whipping pink
with plates of nursery angles
over the strip mines, over
the tasseled corn.

I bore the burden of plums
and pears. My aunt boiled
water for tea on a gas flame,
leaving leaves in the sink.
What she read, she never said.
Her hands smelled of sesame.

The guidelines of rose gardens
were never clear to me. Boxes
bloomed into books. Swans paired
and preened. Pumpkins grew
from flat seeds pressed into hills,
fleshing itchy vines over straw.

I slept in the slanting sun,
strung in numb Sundays.
The horizon was never a straight line,
but oak and hickory heads
and waiting, mites in the light
with yellow bells, calico.

He fed seaweed to sheep.
He drove into deep snow.
He split logs with his metal edge
and drove it hard, down.
I corded the wood
when he was done.

Inland

She tells him stories of crystals dried
on her feet, and that was how they met,
with sand words of gulls and sunlight
and her recall of every shore.

With fingers of desire, wet, sometimes
turning, he brings her back to now,
a thousand miles from any sea. She rows
back to the moon and its ways that pull

her body into patterns, even this far from
urchin, lion, whale, star, and the pearl
that mills in her heels after she goes. Wood
blanches in mighty piles, bark worn off

to heartwood, white and deaf in the roaring stones
tossed back and forth in the Pacific, alone,
or the Atlantic, more quiet and silver. She
has known those shores. Now, in the heart

of the country, she stays with him, with arm
and limb and memory on memory like loam,
here in the continent where the ocean
once reached. She will bring it here again.

Galette des Rois

As the fibers
in blown glass,
like Alabama
tides, yellow fever,
the orphans abide.
They dream
of being brides.

Gabrielle
from St. Denis
sails on the Pelican
from France
with the other girls,
to Mobile
by way of Havana.
She is one
of the last to marry.

The wheat can't
grow with the rust
from the heat,
the humidity
of the bayou,
so they move
the colony upriver.

Farther beyond
in Illinois country,
her son engineers
Fort de Chartres
from river stone
in the limestone heart

of the continent,
for lead and wheat,
the powder magazine.

Her granddaughter
marries a fur trader,
who becomes
lieutenant governor.
The rivers advance
past his walnut bed
and hand-pressed panes.

Don't ever think
that water dreams.
The river rolls
and will not sleep,
but each woman moves
as steam rising.
In the galette des rois,
one small seed
is found.

Confessions

Slate Gray

Sipping Coronas on a dock that cloudy evening in Edmonds was the last time I saw him, his curly brown hair filled with strands of silver. He was waxing philosophical – and why not – he only had a month left. His new liver wasn't working any better than his old one. He said his marriage had failed because of different values, but he liked the freedom. The houses, cars, and degrees didn't mean much. I remember his exact words: In the end what you remember most is the loving you've done in your life. And what you regret the most is not loving more. We leaned on the rail, watching a group of buffleheads dive and return.

Burnt Orange

Just after sunrise you and I sat on the back porch of my apartment on George Washington Way, the neighbor's cat rubbing against my legs and purring, enjoying how I stroked the sides of her neck and under her chin. But the space between us was a chasm. The night before I'd told you about my recurring nightmare: how I was driving across the country to my home town of Peoria and had picked you up hitchhiking, how we took a detour, you showed me your neighborhood, and I ended up locked in a glass museum. I always woke up in a sweat. I needed to be alone. The end of your cigarette glowed as you took another deep drag.

Moonglow

After we put our clothes back on, we parted with a lingering hug, a dance to the rhythm and blues of the Breitenbush River below. The scent of the meadow hot springs buzzed in my head; it must have been 2 or 3 AM. We had soaked together for hours behind the mask of darkness. She hadn't told me her name, but she'd revealed a lot about her life: how she worked behind a glass window because the money was easy, how she undressed in front of men all day and watched them jerk-off, their eyes fixed on her. We talked for hours about sex, our understandings, our confessions – secrets I've never shared with anyone.   It was easy in the darkness with a stranger. The moonlight made our bodies look immortal.

Sequoia Nagamatsu

Giving Howard Junker the Last Word

For twenty-five years, Howard Junker manned the helm of ZYZZYVA, the well-regarded literary journal he started in a San Francisco garage in 1985. During his tenure, he published some of the first stories of writers such as F.X. Toole (Million Dollar Baby), Haruki Murakami (first English translation), Sherman Alexie, and Po Bronson. And this commitment to showcasing emerging talent in addition to the already established continues under the new editors, Laura Cogan and former San Francisco Chronicle Book Reviews Editor and former McSweeney's Publisher, Oscar Villalon. We talk about his retirement from editing, reflections on his long editorial career, his book born from a blog, and what comes next.

SN: I first encountered ZYZZYVA in 2002 at the now closed Borders across from Union Square. As with most chain bookstores, the literary journal offerings were slim. The latest issue of Ploughshares, Zoetrope: All-Story, a few copies of The Sun. And ZYZZYVA. What drew me first to the journal was the name, which I mistook for a complicated abbreviation of something until I found out it was the name of a weevil, the last word in some dictionaries. What stood out to me was the attention given to new writers in the "first time in print" section and the fact that the journal focused on west coast writers and artists. How did you come to decide to specifically showcase emerging West Coast writers and artists? And do you think, in this day and age, there is unique flavor to the art being produced in the west?

HJ: The boundaries of where writers could live evolved gradually. At first, it was going to be an in-house venture, a kind of employees pastime at the big corporation where I worked. There weren't enough warm bodies, so I extended it: the next identity was as The Downtown Review. Still a little sparse, but also, as I looked at the field, I felt that aside from the Threepenny Review the West Coast didn't have a flagship journal,something that could stand up with the litmags of the East, the South, and the Midwest.

I never required the writers to do anything but live in my hood. I think living here is different that living in other places, but there are lots of different kinds of writers living everywhere. And of writer moving around. Or trying different things.

SN: You're about a year into your retirement and have published a collection of your blog posts from 2006-2010, An Old Junker: A Senior Represents. The book comprises of rants, reviews, cultural observations, and the immediacy of thought characteristic of blogs. Our media rich world forces us to live very fractured and piece-meal lives, multi-tasking constantly. In many ways, this book can be seen as a modern collage of a lit mag editor's life. But unlike the blog itself, there's a finality to the posts in book form. There are no comments, no interactivity except in the mind of the reader. You, in fact, have the last word. Can you tell me about the impetus for collecting your blog posts into a book? What do you hope reader will take away from it?

My impetus was to preserve a bit of myself. When I was closing up the office for retirement, I printed out my daily blog and I found that it added up, 1,500 pages, about a foot high. And it seemed to have some good stuff in it. So, since I'm an editor, I thought I would try to put it together.

But I have no hopes for the reader. It's not an ingratiating book. It may not even be a legit book at all. It was the best I could do, the best takes I had during a five-year period. The reason it's sort of a novel is that there is no set form for the novel; the genre is forgiving and all-inclusive. As I try to put it on the back cover, which is, in its way, a parody of back-cover texts:

Bildungsroman would overstate the case, but "diary" seems quotidian. Hipsters might allow that his kaleidoscopic time capsule, distilled from 1,306 posts over five years, 2006-2010, is a blognovel—or bricolage, "a technique," says Wikipedia, "where works are constructed from various materials available or on hand. These materials may be mass-produced or junk."

SN: Your book spans the tail end of your career, but I've been wanting to ask you about the trajectory that brought you to editing in the first place and then to found a literary magazine far from your East Coast roots. Your bios on various websites has given me some highlights (Naval Air Reserve in TN, Newsweek, science teacher, fondue cook), but I want to hear the story in your own words. What drew you to editing? What circumstances led you to found a literary magazine?

Ah, you'd like a mini-memoir. I had started a pretty good career as a magazine journalist in my twenties, freelancing for The Nation, Esquire... and working as an arts writer at Newsweek. Then I got a fellowship at Stanford and decided my next step was in TV documentary. I got a job in San Francisco for a local station but was quickly fired. It took me a a long time, more then ten years, to find my way back. But I had some things i had to do: I needed to work as a carpenter and contractor and as a teacher, because those had been my father's careers. When I was working in the public relations department at Bechtel, a giant engineering-construction firm known especially for its work in nuclear power, I was befriended the department's proofreader, who once, over lunch in the grim corporate cafeteria, told me he had had a literary magazine in Cleveland in the early fifties, publishing Olson & Creeley, Carlos Williams, Ferlinghettii.... I thought, we could do that, too. It took three years—and getting laid off again—before

I launched. It was a desperate effort at self-redemption, at finding something I could do that I would be proud of.

SN: I remember reading an interview you did where you talked about the process of picking stories from the slush pile and working with writers. Many literary magazines don't work with writers extensively due to time/resource issues (esp. those housed at MFA programs), so your level of involvement seemed unique and admirable. And then I found out for myself when I got a phone call from you one day regarding a story. Are there any particular moments during your editing career that are especially memorable to you? A writer you discovered? Difficulties? First triumphs? The just plain strange/weird (apart from the often humorous cover letters you printed on the back of issues)?

At first, I just wanted to publish as many famous writers as I could. And I did cover the scene pretty well. Then I realized that established writers didn't really care whether I published them or not—they had other outlets—but that new writers did need me. So I began to concentrate on them. Over the years, I offered 250 writers their first time in print. That was exciting for them—and for me. I published Kay Ryan in my second issue. Sherman Alexie while he was still an undergraduate. Excerpts from the notebooks that became Under the Tuscan Sun. Haruki Murakami's first story translanted into English. My personal favorite discovery was F.X. Toole, when he was 69—sadly, he died just before Clint Eastwood bought the stories that became Million Dollar Baby.

I had a chance to discover Jonathan Lethem; he was working in a bookstore in Berkeley and sent me a science fiction story; I asked him to work on it a little, but I couldn't bring myself to like it enough to publish it: that was a tragic mistake, keeping the bar too high. I might have discovered Dave Eggers; I visited him in his chaotic loft when he was doing a little spoofy magazine of his own in the early nineties. I wished I knew how to write for it myself, but it didn't occur to me to ask him to write something for me.

SN: ZYZZYVA is now a couple of issues in under the direction of your former managing editor, Laura Cogan. What are your thoughts on the journal as it enters a new era? Are you still involved in any way?

I have nothing to do with the new regime.

SN: And to wrap up, you've devoted much of your life to the written word, to helping artists and writers. Over the course of your career, you've become somewhat of figure, especially in the San Francisco Bay Area. What's next in store for you?

I wish I knew what was in store for me, besides death. Maybe another book or two. The great thing is that with print-on-demand it takes no investment at all to produce a real "book," if you don't worry about anyone reading it, and why should I? I'm an old man; it's all just gravy for me.

Meanwhile, I'm advising a start-up litmag in Santa Cruz, Catamaran. And I help Quiet Lightning in San Francisco. And I refer potential authors to my publisher, IF SF Publishing.

Sequoia Nagamatsu's work has appeared or is forthcoming in West Branch, ZYZZYVA, The Bellevue Literary Review, Gargoyle, elimae, The New Delta Review, and One World: A Global Anthology of Short Stories (New Internationalist, Oxford). He is currently pursuing an MFA in creative writing at Southern Illinois University - Carbondale.

Apology for an Only Child

A brother is born for adversity
—Proverbs 17:17

My lonely boy, I'll never know
The kind of pain that you must feel
To sleep all night in your own room
No brother in the other bed
To keep you up, plot your demise
Accusing you of his own crimes
Stolen cookies, broken lamps
Instead, you'll sleep the sleep of kings
With no one to disturb your dreams

My poor, poor boy—you'll never know
A crowded back seat on the road
No sister there to kick your feet
To poke your rib, to knock your knee
No twins, no triplets to compete
No mother stomping on the brake
No screeching wheels, no sudden shake
Instead, you'll have the whole back seat
Room to stretch, to lounge, to grieve

That's your lot, I'm sad to say
The burden that you must endure
No mid-life guilt, no old regrets
No failed sibling rivalries
No failed siblings to appease
Instead, your folks will worship you
Each competing for your cheek
We're sad to say that we are done
For us, you'll be the only one

For the Roses

I think of her watching the
last rose petals on a
day like today, say deep
August, browning like
an old rubber doll
she might have left
in an attic in Canada.
I think of her pressing
skin against glass, a sense
of summertime falling,
that sense of fall
that that Sylvia Plath
wrote of. Or maybe some
freeze frame of what
is going, moving on.
I see her pale arms,
sea mist velvet jeans
hugging hips that
never will not be boyish.
In the wind, gone
voices move close
to her cheek bones. In
this frame she could be in
a fancy 30's gown. Some
thing is raw, some thing
is broken. It has to be
a full moon
etching black water.
She has to know that
from what is torn

and scarred, some
thing almost too
exquisitely beautiful
is already stirring,
some thing dark
as coal becoming
diamond, insistent,
dying to be born

For the Roses

Sometimes I think of her
as a wild foal, hardly
touching down in prairie
glass, Saskatewan. Or a
sea nymph, her gaze
glued to the deepest
emerald wave, a Silkie
luring men she can't stay
with long. There she
is, on a seaweed jeweled
rock, her songs, ribbons
of melancholy lassoing you,
pulling on your heart.
Some say Bessie Smith
left even or especially good
men to have something
to make her songs
burn the hottest blues. I
think of Joni knowing
what can't stay, what is so
broken it catches the
light like torn bottles
the ocean's turned
to sea glass jewels, that
what dissolves
behind you in the rear
view mirror haunts,
knife- like as her trees,
slashes of wild paint
shivering in a naked row,
such exquisite beauty
in wreckage

Lyn Lifshin

Paprika Plains

I think of her going
backward in time,
back to her home
town floating off
film run backward
until her gray and
blond hair goes
sun and she's wide
eyed to everything.
She's in her mother's
arms and still it
keeps raining. I
imagine Jungle
Gardenia on her
fingers and thumbs
as the moon wanes
and waxes, I think of
her with time
ripped away

Dreamland

I think of her blonde
hair bleached, nearly
snow. Sun scorched
and her skin smelling
of coconut. I think
of island dreams,
sambas and trumpets,
heat dazed, dream
fazed, a lover's
tongue, a glass of
run. Island colors,
guava, rose, peach and
avocado. Drunk on
sun and carnival music.
Licorice skin swaying.
Gambling and rambling.
White snow drifts
6 feet in New York City

Tim Suermondt

Linen White

I attacked the bathroom,
getting, miraculously, more paint
on the walls than on myself—
so deft were my brushstrokes
that, for an instant, I believed
I might have missed my calling,
been another Vermeer.
Then I remembered the joke
'It is a small world,
but I wouldn't want to paint it'
and concluded my self-congratulation
was mocking me. Enough painting.
I washed up, stepped out
to a darkening afternoon,
walked down Majestic and Warsaw,
thinking of a single shaft of light—
beautiful, beautiful Delft.

Tim Suermondt

On Hudson Street

A tiny plaque on a bench,
purchased by the mother
to honor the daughter.

Never mind that the cobblestones
could stand a cleaning,
that the ugly gate surrounding

the ugly parking lot
is too close for comfort
and ideal contemplation—

the April sun covers over
a lot of sins and both the living
and the dead are gearing

for another Spring, the sight
of the coming cherry blossoms
in everyone's mind.

The bench is brown and sturdy,
sturdy as the daughter was,
as the mother is.

Tim Suermondt

Storming The Barricades

With a book of poems in each hand—
what did you expect?
This will make things far less bloody
and give honor to our aggression.
Even the defeated will have to admit:
"Those are some beautiful poems
you beat us with."

Thresholds

The Tuesday evening (seven sharp, please) meetings of the "Fear of Doorways" support group are always sparsely attended. Few show up. Empty chairs scattered around the room, the coffee urn always full, the untouched ashtrays, the many words of worry never uttered. By anyone.

To be frank, no one ever comes. Except myself. In the beginning, I was smart (selfish?) enough to start the group, aware that many others shared my phobia, sure that very few if any would actually appear in my small apartment. Another, subsidiary fear has always been that many would show up, too many, maybe a hundred fellow fearers. If it happened, where would I put them? How would I manage to smile and greet them? Would some, the truly unfortunate, be trampled by the panicked hordes? Would I die too?

Because of the primary fear of doorways, no one has ever come. Some have sent emails. Others have phoned. Some, I feel sure, wrote letters but were, unfortunately, unable to leave their homes to mail the letters at the post office. These communications, received and not, were a comfort, but only to a point. It is never the real thing - the gathering together, the bodies huddled shoulder to twitchy shoulder in irrational dread. The sweat, the cramped body language, the overused toilet room - none of it has happened.

I watch the door, which is open. No one crosses the threshold. No one will. And I will remain inside, unable to venture forth.

At nine (sharp, please respect the rules), I adjourn. I close down the meeting. I do not move. I would turn off the light but electrical switches are a third-tier fear. I close my eyes, hope to rest. But the terror I associate with my brutal, even vicious dreams keeps me awake, unwilling to risk much needed sleep. So I remain vigilant, consider the meeting now done, begin to think about next week's meeting (seven sharp, please).

Contributors

PINCKNEY BENEDICT is the author of four volumes of fiction, the most recent of which is *Miracle Boy and Other Stories*. He is a professor on the faculty of the creative writing program at Southern Illinois University Carbondale.

CLIFFORD GARSTANG, a former international lawyer, earned his MFA from Queens University of Charlotte. His award-winning linked story collection, *In an Uncharted Country*, was published in 2009. A novel in stories, *What the Zhang Boys Know*, is forthcoming in 2012 from Press 53. Recent work has appeared or is forthcoming in *Blackbird, Bellevue Review, Cream City Review, Los Angeles Review, Tampa Review*, and elsewhere. He is the Editor of *Prime Number Magazine*.

NINA SCHUYLER is the author of *The Painting*, which was a finalist for the Northern California Book Award, and translated into Chinese, Japanese, Portuguese, Serbian, and Accidental Birds (forthcoming, 2012). Her short stories have been published in *ZYZZYVA, Fugue, Santa Clara Review, Stanford Magazine*. Two stories have been nominated for Pushcart Prize. She's the fiction editor at ablemuse.com. and teaches creative writing at the University of San Francisco.

JESSICA BARKSDALE is the author of twelve novels (some under Jessica Inclan), including *Her Daughter's Eyes, The Matter of Grace*, and *When You Believe*. She is a Professor of English at Diablo Valley College and teaches online novel writing for UCLA Extension.

DEIDRE WOOLLARD is a fiction writer living in Los Angeles. She received her M.F.A. from Spalding University. Her stories have appeared in *Sojourn, Big Ugly Review, Dirt Press, Pebble Lake Review*, the *Mota IV* anthology, *Words and Images*, and on the SNReview.org and StoryGlossia.com websites. She won second place in the Andre Dubus Prize for Short Fiction 2004, second in the Confluence Fiction Contest 2003, third place in the Clark College Contest 2004 and was nominated for a Pushcart Prize in 2005.

JILL STUKENBERG's recent fiction has appeared in *Prick of the Spindle, The Florida Review*, and *Penduline Press*. A graduate of the MFA program at New Mexico State University, she currently teaches at University of Wisconsin-Marathon County, where she hosts the creative writing reading series 1,000 Words Wausau.

CHRISTOPHER WOODS is a writer, teacher and photographer who lives in Texas. He has published a novel, *The Dream Patch*, a prose collection, *Under a Riverbed Sky*, and a book of stage monologues for actors, *Heart Speak*. His photo essays have appeared in a number of publications including *Glasgow Review, Public Republic* and *Narrative Magazine*.

ROSIE FORREST holds her MFA in Fiction from the University of New Hampshire, where she received both the Thomas Williams and Dick Shea Memorial Awards for her stories. As a teacher, she has taught creative writing at UNH and is a summer writing faculty member for Interlochen Arts Camp. Most recently, Rosie's flash fiction appeared on *Cheek Teeth*, the online mouthpiece for *Trachodon Magazine*. She is currently at work on her short story collection, *Hush Hush, Old Girl*.

JOHN G. RODWAN JR., is the author of *Fighters & Writers* (Mongrel Empire Press, 2010), a collection of pugilistic literary essays, and *Christmas Things* (Monkey Puzzle Press, forthcoming), a nonfiction chapbook. His writing has been published by *The American Interest, The Mailer Review, Blood and Thunder, Spot Literary Magazine, The Nevada Review, The Oregonian, Philip Roth Studies, Palimpsest, Fight News, Free Inquiry, The Humanist and Secular World*, among other journals, magazines and newspapers. He was raised in Detroit, Michigan, and in 2011, after fifteen years during which he lived in Geneva, Switzerland; Brooklyn, New York; and Portland, Oregon, he returned to his hometown.

PAMELA BALLUCK's creative writing has appeared in, among other publications, *Western Humanities Review, The Southeast Review, Barrow Street, Pank, Night Train, Avery Anthology, Freight*

Stories, and is forthcoming in *Robert Olen Butler Prize Stories*. "In The Briefcase Veronica Gave Me After Grace Died" is from a creative nonfiction book in progress, *Self Storage*. She teaches writing at the University of Utah in Salt Lake City, where she earned her M.F.A. and Ph.D. in fiction.

JESSICA ERICA HAHN has her writing published in *The Tonopah Review, Ontologica: A Journal of Art and Thought, Wordrunner, Bread & Lightning, Genepoetry,* and has several self-published books from the 1990s, when she was a college dropout who hopped freight trains and lived in abandoned buildings around the United States. She is currently writing a novel about seafaring hippies, which just won the Clark-Gross Award in the Novel at San Francisco State University. She is the recipient of two upcoming writing residencies, one at the Andrews Experimental Forest in Oregon, while the other is a Red Gate Residency in Beijing, China. She lives in San Francisco. Please visit her website at jessicaericahahn.com

THEODORE WOROZBYT's work has appeared or is forthcoming in *Antioch Review, Crazyhorse, The Iowa Review, New England Review, Po&sie, Poetry, Sentence, Shenandoah, The Southern Review, TriQuarterly Online* and *Quarterly West*. He has published two books of poetry, *The Dauber Wings* (Dream Horse Press, 2006) and *Letters of Transit*, which won the 2007 Juniper Prize (The University of Massachusetts Press, 2008). He is an assistant professor of English at Georgia Perimeter College.

LYN LIFSHIN has written more than 125 books and edited 4 anthologies of women writers. Her poems have appeared in most poetry and literary magazines in the U.S.A, and her work has been included in virtually every major anthology of recent writing by women. She has given more than 700 readings across the U.S.A. and has appeared at Dartmouth and Skidmore colleges, Cornell University, the Shakespeare Library, Whitney Museum, and Huntington Library. She has also taught poetry and prose writing for many years at universities, colleges and high schools, and has been Poet in Residence at the University of Rochester, Antioch, and Colorado Mountain College. Winner of numerous awards including the Jack Kerouac Award for her book *Kiss The Skin Off*, She is the subject of the documentary film *Lyn Lifshin: Not Made of Glass*. She has been praised by Robert Frost, Ken Kesey and Richard Eberhart, and Ed Sanders has seen her as "a modern Emily Dickinson."

AMY SCHREIBMAN WALTER was born in Florida. She now lives in London, where she has recently completed a course of study at the Faber Poetry Academy. Her poems have been published on both sides of the Atlantic. You can find her at www. amyschreibmanwalter.com

CHANGMING YUAN, (co-)author of *Chansons of a Chinaman* (2009) and *Three Poets* (2001) as well as a 4-time Pushcart nominee, grew up in rural China and published several monographs before moving to North America. With a Canadian PhD in English, Yuan teaches independently in Vancouver and has poetry appearing in 420 literary publications across 18 countries, including *Barrow Street, Best Canadian Poetry, BestNewPoemsOnline, London Magazine, Poetry Kanto, Poetry Salzburg, Taj Mahal Review* and *Yuan Yang*.

ANGIE MACRI was born and raised in southern Illinois. Her recent work appears in *The Carolina Quarterly, The Pinch*, and *Third Coast*, among other journals, and is included in *Best New Poets 2010*. A recipient of an individual artist fellowship from the Arkansas Arts Council, she teaches in Little Rock.

LOIS MARIE HARROD won the 2010 Hazel Lipa Chapbook (Iowa State University) contest with her manuscript *Cosmogony* and her 11th book *Brief Term*, a collection of poems about teachers and teaching was published by Black Buzzard in March 2011. She teaches Creative Writing at The College of New Jersey.

GEORGE SUCH is a graduate student studying English at Western Washington University in Bellingham, Washington; in a previous incarnation he was a chiropractor for twenty-seven years in eastern Washington. His poems have appeared in *Arroyo Literary Review, Blue Earth Review, Cold Mountain Review, Crab Creek Review, Dislocate, Permafrost, Roanoke Review, The Sow's Ear Poetry Review*, and several other journals.

JAY RUBIN teaches writing at The College of Alameda in the San Francisco Bay Area, where he's publishes *Alehouse*, an all-poetry literary journal, at www.alehousepress.com. He holds an MFA in Poetry from New England College and lives in San Francisco with his son and Norwich terrier.

KIRBY WRIGHT was born and raised in Honolulu, Hawaii. He is a graduate of Punahou School in Honolulu and the University of California at San Diego. He received his MFA in Creative Writing from San Francisco State University. Wright has been nominated for two Pushcart Prizes and is a past recipient of the Ann Fields Poetry Prize, the Academy of American Poets Award, the Browning Society Award for Dramatic Monologue, and Arts Council Silicon Valley Fellowships in Poetry and The Novel. *Before the City*, his first book of poetry, took First Place at the 2003 San Diego Book Awards. Wright is also the author of the companion novels *Punahoe Blues* and *Moloka'i Nui Ahina*, both set in Hawaii. He was a Visiting Fellow at the 2009 International Writers Conference in Hong Kong, where he represented the Pacific Rim region of Hawaii.

TIM SUERMONDT has published two chapbooks and two full-length collections of poems, *Trying To Help The Elephant Man Dance* from Backwaters Press, 2007, and *Just Beautiful* from New York Quarterly Books, 2010. He's had poems in many magazines and online, including: *The Georgia Review, Poetry, Poetry East, Blackbird, Poetry Northwest, Atlanta Review and Bellevue Literary Review*, with poems forthcoming in *Southern Humanities Review, Prairie Schooner* and *Stand Magazine* (U.K.) among others. He has poems in *Poetry after 9/11: An Anthology of New York Poets* (Melville House Publications, 2002) and *Visiting Walt* (a Whitman anthology from the University of Iowa Press, 2003.) He lives in Brooklyn with his wife, the poet Pui Ying Wong.

NANCY COOK currently teaches, writes, and parents in the Minneapolis/St Paul area. She holds an M.F.A . from American University and a law degree from Georgetown, and has spent much of the last fifteen years attempting to integrate the various parts of herself. Her work has appeared or is forthcoming in a variety of literary and social policy journals, including *adventum, Florida Review, Southern Anthology, Virginia Journal of Social Policy, Westward Quarterly* and *Harvard Women's Law Journal*.

CATHY KODRA's poetry and short stories have appeared or are forthcoming in *Slow Trains, Roanoke Review, Birmingham Arts Journal, Common Ground Review, Cavalier Literary Couture, Opium, Still Crazy, New Millennium Writings, The Medulla Review*, and others. She is a contributing editor for New Millennium Writings and the current guest poetry editor for *The Medulla Review*.

DONNA COFFEY is an Associate Professor of English at Reinhardt University. She holds a Ph.D. in English from the University of Virginia and an MFA in Creative Writing from the Solstice Program at Pine Manor College. Her academic work has appeared in *Women's Studies: An Interdisciplinary Journal, Modern Fiction Studies, Science as Culture, Contemporary Women's Writing*, and the collection *Holocaust Text and National Context*, forthcoming in 2012. Her poetry has appeared or is forthcoming in *Calyx, qarrtsiluni, The Honey Land Review* and *The Comstock Review*.

MARY CHRISTINE DELEA is from Long Island and now lives in Oregon. Her fourth book of poems, *Did I Mention There's Gambling and Body Parts?*, will be published by dancing girl press in 2012. She is currently teaching ESL to Russian speakers and working on two nonfiction books, as well as some poetry manuscripts.

JEN EDWARDS is a third year Ph.D. student in English at Oklahoma State University where she studied with the Poet Ai and currently studies with Lisa Lewis. Her work has previously appeared in such journals as *The Laurel Review, Compass Rose*, and *The Monarch Review*. She received an AWP Intro Award nomination in 2011.